Through the Eyes of Ernest

A Memoir to Honor Elephants

DEBBIE MCFEE

D1372194

ISBN: 1492703796
ISBN 13: 9781492703792

This book is dedicated to Pat Derby and Karl Cullen who left us way too soon.

CONTENTS

Author's Note

THE PURPOSE OF this book is to raise awareness and educate the reader about the amazing complexity of elephants. And how we, mankind, have not done right by them. I also want to remind the reader that we have a choice in whether or not we keep elephants, or any animal, captive. The elephants do not have a choice.

Ernest's story is a well researched fictional account of real life events. Ernest represents *Every Elephant*. There are currently three species of elephants in the world: Asian Elephants, African Savanna Elephants, and African Forest Elephants. For the purpose of this story, it does not matter which species. This book is about any and all elephants who have lived or currently live captive to man in North America. Elephants are not indigenous to North America and true conservation of elephants in other countries is approached differently.

Elephants are extremely intelligent, kind, sensitive, and gentle beings who experience joy, happiness, forgiveness, and love. They are also capable of boredom, loneliness, frustration, grief, and even despair. They function in a highly sophisticated and organized society led by an older and wiser matriarch. They are extremely social and help one another in giving birth and raising their young. Females stay with their families for life. Elephants communicate vocally, sometimes with sounds inaudible to humans and seismically through the ground. They honor their dead. When a friend or family member dies, the other elephants stay with the body and mourn. They weep real tears.

Elephants are everything we can ever hope to be. They are already there. We can learn a lot from our Elephant friends. If only we would listen…

DAM

ACKNOWLEDGEMENTS

ERNEST'S STORY WOULD not be possible without the hard work of Carol Buckley, Scott Blais, the late Pat Derby, Ed Stewart, Joyce Poole, Ian Douglas-Hamilton, Catherine Moss, David and Daphne Sheldrick, Lek Chailert, Katherine Connor, Louise Rogerson, the late Karl Cullen, the late Lawrence Anthony, and Katy Payne. There are so many incredible people on the front lines helping the elephants, far too many to mention here.

Special thanks to John Fowles, F. Scott Fitzgerald, and Lillian Hellman whose writing greatly influenced my writing. And special thanks to Gay Bradshaw, Christopher Nicholson, Cleveland Amory, Anna Sewall and Lyall Watson whose writing and research greatly influenced this book.

For those who want to learn more about elephants, a suggested reading list is at the back of the book. Visit Ernest's web page at *www.4theelephants.com/Organizations* if you want to learn more about how to help elephants.

SPECIAL THANKS

A SPECIAL THANK you to Janice Buckwalter, Doug and Courtney McFee, Robbie and Patty Robertson, Stephen Ramras, Dave Elder, Tom Brown, Shawn McDonald, Roz McCreery, Wendy Bell, Tommy Kyle, Susan Berlin, Mike and Maureen McCarthy, Jeff Ramras, Michael Clague, and Randy Blackmon for believing in Ernest's story.

And to Laura Seager, John McFee, Dan Haley, Eileen Kulp, Jen Adriany, Derek Beatty, Nick Kepics, Kevin Hodgson, Tom Flake, Clint Mitchell, Jiffy and Danny Childress, George Thompson, Susan Avinger, Robert Chromy, Charlene Herrala, Karen Williams, Joanna Bickham, and Corky Condon for helping to make Ernest's story a reality.

COVER PHOTO

THE COVER PHOTO was taken by me at Buffalo Springs Game Reserve, in Samburu, Kenya, June, 2013. Two bulls crossed the Ewaso Nyiro River to our camp for the vegetation. I could tell by the size of their tusks that they were young adult bulls. May they grow up to be big and strong and live long and happy lives!

For the elephants...

PROLOGUE

ONE OF MY first clear memories is when I discovered a large growth on my face. It came out from below my eyes and was extremely long. I was not sure what to do with it and tripped over it constantly. Sometimes I would suck on it for comfort when I felt unsure of myself. My mother had one too and she hugged me with it often. I found out later, it was an extension of my upper lip and nose. My mom told me it was very muscular and had many functions. She referred to it as a trunk.

I remember a large fenced-in area with hard dirt and small patches of grass. Or so it seemed big from my perspective at the time. The warmth of my mother's gigantic body and the sweet smell of hay and dung are forever etched in my memory. My trunk breathed in her scent and I loved the texture of her soft wrinkly skin. I could never get enough of her and never left her side as I suckled on and off throughout the day. I loved to nuzzle up against her and fall asleep in the straw at night or during the day when we both napped. Other times, when I leaned against her strong, sturdy body I could feel her heartbeat. I remember my mother ate nonstop, most days over 150 pounds of hay, vegetables, and fruit. I watched her use her trunk to pick up the food she put into her mouth. Most days she drank over 50 gallons of water! Eventually, she showed me how to fill my trunk with water and then transfer it to my mouth. She also used it to pull clumps of grass from the ground. It would take me years to master the use of my trunk. In the meantime, I was happy to suckle.

Another female accompanied my mother. I could tell they were good friends because they hugged several times during the day and before we lay down to sleep at night. She and my mother hung out a lot. I cannot remember her name, but she made a big deal over me, always wanting to touch me with her trunk. I did not mind and actually enjoyed the attention, but always preferred the warmth and safety of my mom. On hot days we enjoyed the shade of a large canopy. When I was very young, I stood underneath my mother as she flapped her massive ears to stay cool. Before sundown each day, the three of us headed toward a barn-like shelter for the evening meal and stayed chained until after the sun came up the next morning. On cool nights we huddled together for warmth. I remember watching their huge sides rise and fall with each breath as I rested my body against their warm, soft skin. I loved to listen to the strong slow beating of my mother's heart when I pressed my ear against her side. Sometimes the hairs on her legs tickled my face. Her warm breath wafted softly on my cheek or ear as I fell off to sleep at night. Each day drifted and melted into the next. A happy time for me, the only life I knew.

A few months after I turned three, something happened and my life changed forever. When we returned to the shelter and chained for our evening meal, some men I had never seen before came into our area. No longer small enough to fit underneath my mom, I hid behind her eight-thousand-pound body as they stared at me. The men walked toward us and my mom growled a low warning. Her friend stood sideways to block the men from us. I remember feeling my mother's fear. Her hairs stood on end and her heart thundered loudly. She and her friend emitted low rumbles back and forth. Five men with dark weathered faces held long wooden sticks and had ropes and chains thrown over their shoulders. One of the men with a dark scowl etched deep into his face carried a dart gun. It happened so fast and I cannot remember every detail. I do remember my mother's deep guttural noises really scared me. Two of the men struck her face and my mother screamed and roared, everything after that a blur. I remember my legs being tied together and I could not move. My mother and her friend bellowed, roared, trumpeted, and screamed. Then total darkness…

My name is Ernest, and I am a seven-ton, forty-five-year-old bull elephant. This is my story. In order to tell my story, I must first tell you theirs.

1

FRANKIE

And in the sweetness of friendship let there be laughter, and sharing of pleasures. For in the dew of little things the heart finds its morning and is refreshed.
—KHALIL GIBRAN

I AWAKENED TO find myself in an unfamiliar place. Groggy, I cried out for my mother. The ground felt cold and damp. Moonlight revealed gray walls and barren gray ground. Hungry, cold, and scared, I called out. Silence. I called out to her again, the silence now deafening. I started to cry. I cried until my eyes hurt. I cried until my stomach hurt. I cried and cried, until I had no tears left and was too exhausted to cry anymore. In my wretchedness, I fell asleep on the cold, gray cement floor. I awakened again, this time to the sound of human voices. Two men stood over me. They placed a bucket of water and hay on the floor, looked me over,

1

and abruptly disappeared. More thirsty than hungry, I gulped down the water and soothed my parched throat. When the bucket was almost empty, I devoured the hay and actually enjoyed the taste of it. Using my trunk, I crammed every last piece of hay into my mouth, then finished the water. I knocked the bucket over and trumpeted loudly for my mother. I kicked it around the depressing enclosure, the clanging echoed in the eerie silence. As the bucket began to lose its shape, I became bored with the whole mess. I slammed it against the wall with my trunk when a soft voice rumbled, "Feel better?" Startled, I turned around to see an extremely large elephant. He made my mother who had always seemed enormous to me look tiny. I felt terribly small and insignificant next to this imposing giant. Confused and scared, I faced the oversized elephant.

"Hello," I squeaked. "Who are you?"

"My name is Frankie," he rumbled softly. "What's your name?"

"My name is Ernest," I peeped as I looked at him in awe. "Where are we? I want my mom. I am cold."

"There, there, little fellow, it gets easier. You'll get used to things here."

"Here? Where is here?"

"Why, you are at the zoo."

"What is a zoo?"

"It is a place where humans come to stare at us."

"Why?"

"Because they want to see what we look like."

"Oh," I said, not understanding and sucked my trunk.

From the time I was three until after I turned seven, I lived in a zoo Frankie referred to as *the cement prison*. Frankie and I in separate cells had barely enough room to turn around. We could see and touch each other through the steel bars separating us. The only elephants at the zoo, we became fast friends.

I was inconsolable the first several months and desperately longed for the physical comfort of my mother. I missed her gentleness and her soft rumbles. Every night I cried myself to sleep. Frankie paced in place softly explaining it would get better, the tip of his trunk gently touching my tear-stained face. I did not believe him. What did he know?

Turns out he did know. He had been in the same cell for ten years and just turned twenty when I met him. Prior to coming to the zoo, he spent seven years of his life as the only elephant in a roadside petting zoo. Frankie was born in the wild and taken from his mother when he was three. He understood my devastation all too well. He also had some idea of what it meant to be a wild elephant. He just never got the hang of how to be an elephant all by himself, "Since the whole point of being an elephant is growing up in a close-knit family with lots of friends! An elephant without other elephants is not an elephant," he would grumble, waving his trunk for emphasis.

No interaction with another elephant for seven years. No toys, no one to play with, just food, if you could call it that—some slop in a bucket twice a day. The humans came to stare at him and brought him peanuts. Frankie hated peanuts! He sucked them in his trunk then blew them out all over the spectators who thought him, "Oh, so funny." He believed if the boredom did not kill him the loneliness would. He ended up at the zoo with the label "dangerous elephant."

"Dangerous? Good grief, some idiot human kept poking me with a sharp stick to get me to sit up like a dog. When I refused, he withheld food," Frankie trumpeted and swished his trunk indignantly. "Well, after a while, I grew irritable because the hook on the stupid stick hurt, plus I was always hungry. One day he taunted me to stand on my head and I refused to play his silly little game. He grabbed the underside of my chin with the hook so hard it brought tears to my eyes. Instinctively my head jerked back away from the hook. I cried out in pain and knocked him out with my trunk. He never woke up. I ended up here in isolation for a while. I remember waking up one day from a very deep, unexpected sleep and found myself with all four of my legs chained and barely able to move. Two humans stood on either side of me and beat my body with sharp pointed metal hooks on the end of long sticks for days on end."

Horrified, I stared into his huge handsome face and could only manage to squeak out a pitiful, "Why?"

"Supposedly to make me less aggressive," he shrugged. "Good grief. Anyway, I ended up in this cement prison." He snorted, "I couldn't go to a breeding facility and was considered too dangerous to perform. As one becomes available, the zoo will transfer a baby elephant here so more humans will come and stare at us. I am not enough of an attraction by myself, and I won't play their silly game by performing demeaning tricks. Besides, everyone loves a baby elephant. If we live long enough, they will eventually ship one of us out of here and bring in another baby."

I nodded like I understood, but I had no idea what he meant at the time. The four-plus years I spent with Frankie, I came to know him as a gentle and kindhearted soul. His sheer size made him a formidable force. He weighed almost six tons with tusks over five feet long. And even though Frankie was as tenderhearted as they came and would not even hurt an insect, all but one of the humans who tended to us remained afraid of him.

Mr. William, a tall, thin, extremely gentle man, was horrified when he saw the condition Frankie was in when he first arrived at the zoo to take care of him. He immediately released Frankie from the chains that incapacitated him and gently washed and tended to his wounds from the hook. Mr. William *never* used a stick or hook on Frankie or me. He always spoke kindly to us and tried to make our lives as comfortable as he could. "How comfortable is a cement prison?" Frankie would grumble bitterly. The floor and two of the walls were cement. Thick steel bars faced out toward where the humans stared at us and in between Frankie's enclosure and mine. Never out of view of curious humans, we endured taunting, oohs and ahs, and stares day in and day out. Mr. William brought us fresh hay several times a day and a few times a week he treated us to bamboo branches. Frankie and I looked forward to these treats. Sometimes, after all the humans left for the day, Mr. William brought us bananas. Frankie went bananas over the bananas! One of the only times I saw him smile was when he ate bananas. He chewed ever so slowly and savored every bite. To this day, I cannot see a banana and not think of Frankie.

Frankie taught me the wonders of having a trunk. My mother had shown me how to drink with it and how to stuff food in my mouth. But she did not tell me my trunk had over 40,000 muscles and could lift about 700 pounds. Frankie said, "That would be like lifting three big men or two very fat ones!" Sometimes when Frankie was tired, he would rest his trunk over one of his tusks when it became too heavy. I could not do that at the time because my tusks were too short. He would tell me stories about how his family would tear the bark and break large branches off the trees with a single pull of their trunks. The adults would reach high up the tree to get the really tasty leaves. In the wild, his family used the tip of their trunks to suck dirt and then raise their trunks overhead to blow dirt all over their backs. This helped ward off insects and protect their sensitive skin from the sun. It bothered Frankie he was unable to dust-bathe. He would grumble about the insects at the zoo especially in the summer. He never had to worry about sun burn because he never saw the sun the entire time he was in the *cement prison*!

When I was five, three human boys approached us. They stared at Frankie. Then started laughing and pointing at him. He slowly chewed some hay as he watched them watch him. They thought it funny to hurl sticks at him, small ones at first, then larger ones. Frankie, unaffected, continued to eat. Frustrated by his lack of reaction, they threw stones at him. One missed and hit me. It felt like a sharp object had been jammed in my face and I backed up a bit. The boys laughed. Why were they were so mean? I know the stones had to hurt Frankie, but he never flinched. I was wondering how he could just stand there when I heard a loud thunk. Two of the boys ran away. The other one fell. Mr. William had whacked him on the back of the head with a shovel. I heaved a huge sigh of relief and Frankie snorted, "Serves him right!" Mr. William always looked out for us, as there was no place for us to go to get away from the onslaught of rocks or humans. I could tell by the way he and Frankie looked at each other how much they loved each other. He always referred to him as "Frankie, old boy." Frankie and I happily did whatever Mr. William asked. Frankie once told me, "Mr. William believes all beings should be treated with kindness and respect."

One day, Frankie told me about the ways of the humans. "There are many types of humans," he rumbled. "There are good, kind, thoughtful humans like Mr. William, who genuinely care about us and our well-being. Then there are bad, cruel humans who have no business in the company of elephants—or any creature, for that matter. There are also many foolish humans—careless, ineffective, and ignorant to the ways of elephants. They think they are helping us, but they aren't. They don't respect us for who and what we are. I hope you end up in good hands, Ernest. Unfortunately, we never know who will buy us or where we will end up. It is all up to chance for us. Just remember to enjoy whatever kindness comes your way."

After I turned seven, Frankie started complaining about his feet and his leg joints. They had deteriorated from years of standing on the unforgiving cement and caused him severe pain and discomfort. He would try to walk in place by crossing one foot in front of the other and back and forth to relieve the pain. Since I was smaller, I had more room to walk around in my cell. He always encouraged me to keep moving in order to save my feet and legs. I must admit, we looked quite comical as we danced around in our prison cells! One rainy afternoon while we enjoyed some freshly cut bamboo from Mr. William, Frankie rumbled, "Oh how my body misses standing on soft dirt in lush green pastures where I can stretch my legs. I long to feel the warmth of the sun on my back while I drink from clear, still waters! At least I have my dreams of rivers of cool water to bathe in," he sighed wistfully. "I miss my family and friends. I want to roam free and feed on fresh green leaves and grass. Ernest, always remember to be kind to others. The world of humans is one I don't care to understand. Remember how much your mother loves you, and know we are greatly missed even though we are far away from our families. I have enjoyed our friendship these past years and will never forget you." He reached through the bars and affectionately touched my face with his trunk. Later in the afternoon, while the sun tried to peek through the clouds, I heard Frankie grumbling. At first I thought he was talking in his sleep and I walked over to the bars separating us. His back leaned against the cement wall. As he faced me, he grumbled loudly and agitatedly. "Good grief, I can't get up. My legs don't have the strength!" He laid his head down. That was the last time I ever saw him alive.

***

HE LAY IN his cement cell for three days before the humans removed his body. I stared at his body and cried for hours on end. I begged him to come back. I reached through the bars, touched him with my trunk, and desperately tried to coax him back to life. It was Frankie, but not Frankie. His brown eyes stared blindly from his handsome face, the face I had grown to love deeply. I could not believe Frankie was gone. I still cannot. Mr. William was devastated, in tears over losing Frankie. They had been together ten years before I arrived. To make matters worse, Mr. William disappeared after Frankie's body was taken away. Maybe he blamed himself for Frankie's death, I do not know. Looking back, I realize now, Frankie was saying good-bye. I believe he chose to die. What kind of life did he have? He wanted to do something on his own terms. Not having been able to in life, meant dying on his terms. Rest in peace, my friend. I am a better elephant for having known you.

***

NOT SURE WHICH was more excruciatingly painful without Frankie—the loneliness or the boredom. Having never been alone, I missed sharing our morning meals, our long talks about anything and everything, his irritability, his stories, his kind gentle spirit, and his wisdom. And more than anything, I missed the way he hugged me with his huge trunk through the bars at night when we slept. I missed his gentle snoring and warm breath as I fell off to sleep. I thought a lot about my mother in the months following Frankie's death. I missed her loving rumbles. I wondered if I had any brothers or sisters and if she ever thought about me. Frankie had always been certain his mother thought about him, even after twenty-plus years had passed. "Good grief, how *could* she forget me? I think of her every single day!" he would snort and wave his trunk.

Even when I did not think about my mother, she was always on my mind. I missed talking to Frankie about her. Having someone to talk to about my mom kept her alive for me. I missed the way Frankie's eyes twinkled when he talked about his family, the only other times I saw him smile besides when he was eating bananas. He loved to talk about running around with his younger brother and older sisters, chasing each other, terrorizing the older elephants, stealing his mother's food, knocking down trees, kicking up clouds of dirt while they squealed and trumpeted their little hearts out! "Good grief, how I miss doing elephant things!" he would sigh and grumble softly.

As the hours melted into days, then weeks, and then months, there was no relief from the loneliness and boredom. The isolation became intolerable. I did not have the wherewithal to endure the endless solitary hours. Frankie was right. An elephant without other elephants is not an elephant at all! My new human caretaker, Mr. Joe, was not the least bit interested in my well-being. Completely indifferent to me, he swept out my prison cell only once a week, in contrast to Mr. William's several times a day. There was no place to get away from the stench of urine and dung. I always had plenty of water, but hay only twice a day and no treats. How I craved bamboo and bananas! I wondered what Frankie would have to say about the new human. After six agonizing months, thin and agitated without a good night's sleep since Frankie's death, I decided I did not want to end up like Frankie nor would he have wanted me to. I watched Mr. Joe carelessly open and close my cell many times in those months. With very little effort, I managed to unhook the latch with my trunk.

The ground felt deliciously soft beneath my feet. I started to walk away from my cell and realized I had no idea where I was going, then decided it did not matter where I walked as long as I walked. I walked for Frankie. My legs and feet hurt, but I did not care, it felt so good to stretch my legs. The full moon cast an eerie shadow of my frail, thin body. I walked around the prison for hours and ate fresh grass, drank water out of decorative fountains, and observed all the other incarcerated animals. All were asleep except an old lion who paced dejectedly in his desolate cement cell. He stopped long enough to make eye contact and nod at me, then continued to pace. I made several unsuccessful attempts to unlock his cell. He smiled his appreciation at me with the saddest eyes I have ever seen. His eyes still haunt me today.

I grew tired from walking around the prison for most of the night and went to rest under a tree near the fountain. My stomach full and my body tired, I fell into a deep sleep under the stars.

***

I AWOKE AT dawn ravenously hungry and grazed on some fresh grass. I felt refreshed after my first decent night's sleep since Frankie died. Plus, I had not eaten fresh grass since arriving at the zoo. As I quietly enjoyed my meal I heard a commotion behind me. I turned to see several humans frantically waving their arms and pointing at the elephant enclosure. I finished my breakfast and walked over to a fountain and filled my trunk with water all the while enjoying my freedom. As the other prisoners awakened and loudly demanded breakfast, I decided to head over to my cell when Mr. Joe and four other humans I did not know surrounded me. They beat me with sharp hooks and I thought of Frankie, the "dangerous" elephant. He was right. Those pointy-ended sticks hurt! Feeling a little frisky, I ran ahead into my cement cell. I heard the door slam behind me and watched Mr. Joe carelessly latch the lock.

For several months I let myself out at night after the humans went home for the day. I enjoyed my nocturnal adventures. I ate plenty of delicious grass and it was fun to drink out of the different fountains. On hot balmy nights I filled my trunk with water and sprayed it all over myself to cool off. I walked around the zoo for hours and visited the other animals. At the first hint of dawn I returned to my cell and after breakfast slept most of the day. I began to gain weight and the exercise made me stronger and healthier.

Right before my eighth birthday a human came to see me. He decided to buy me as a companion pet for his daughter's lonely elephant. According to Mr. Joe, I was a worthless zoo elephant because all I did was sleep during the day. The humans had stopped coming to *look at* me which was bad for business. They loaded me onto the back of a truck and for a full day and night I had no food or water. When I arrived at my new destination I was led into an extremely large fenced-in area with a small barn. As the sun began to peek over the horizon I heard frantic trumpeting and saw a tiny, gray elephant with big floppy ears and a short trunk running toward me. Younger than me and very beautiful, she shyly extended her trunk in greeting.

2

Maggie

"We'll be Friends Forever, won't we, Pooh?"
asked Piglet.
"Even longer," Pooh answered.
—A. A. Milne

Her name was Maggie and she had bright expressive eyes with the most beautiful long eyelashes. She had lived in paradise for almost four years. My stomach rumbled loudly. I was hungry as I had not eaten since the day before. Again she reached out a little shyly, touched me and in a few minutes we headed out across a vast field, trunks entwined. Maggie did not know her mother at all because a human she barely remembered bottle-fed her for a year. She was purchased from a zoo where her young mother rejected her. After she arrived in paradise, Maggie was bottle-fed for two years by Miss Lacey, the twelve-year old daughter of her new owner. Miss Lacey played with her every day and night until recently. The teenager had developed new interests and did not come around as much. We stopped at a grassy area next to a stream and a dense cluster of trees.

"You are here to be my new playmate and keep me company! What is your name?"

"My name is Ernest."

"My name is Maggie. I am almost five. How old are you?"

"I am almost eight."

I watched Maggie bend her front legs to kneel down and lap the water with her mouth from a clear stream. No one had ever shown her how to use her trunk to drink water! I showed her how to fill her trunk with water and then put her trunk in her mouth and drink. She was a fast learner and together we drank away the early morning from an unlimited supply of water. I drank like I never drank before. Maggie raised her trunk and squirted water above her head. Water sprayed all over everything, including me! I enjoyed watching her do this several times before I did the same. Water everywhere, both of us drenched! Maggie mischievously squirted me right in the face and squealed delightedly. Like boisterous children, what a mess we made, and what fun we had! I thought of Frankie and how much he would love this place. How he would love to be able to act the way an elephant ought to. I imagined the three of us as we bellowed loud trumpets of delight and roamed free on acres and acres of lush green grass. No cement anywhere in sight.

I grazed. Maggie observed me grab the grass with my trunk and did the same. How I missed Mr. William's treats of bananas and bamboo branches! I felt a pang and missed Mr. William and Frankie terribly. Frankie had described a place like this to me many times from his memory of the wild, with its lush landscape, tender grasses, acres of trees, and several ponds. Maggie looked up from her grazing and stripped some bark off the nearest tree. Still chewing, she batted her long beautiful eyelashes at me, "This is a new day full of fun and wonderful things. Let's go play in the mud after we eat!"

We dashed over to the pond to wallow in the mud after our late-morning feeding frenzy. Embarrassed, I confessed, "I have never stripped bark off a tree or wallowed in the mud. I have heard all about these activities from my friend Frankie though." Maggie turned out to be a great teacher and so much fun to play with. She made my heart smile. Our trunks reached out to grab branches from trees and tear off the bark which we stuffed into our mouths, nonstop.

Our soon to be morning routine of foraging, mud-wallowing, napping, grazing, and exploring had begun. From this point on, Maggie and I could not keep our trunks off each other. We became inseparable. We squealed and rumbled our happiness to be alive as each day drifted and melted into the next. At night we slept in separate stalls, yet could touch each other and entwine our trunks through the wooden slats dividing us. A small spring glided through the meadow and ran softly by our stable day and night.

I loved to fall asleep to the sound of its gentle rippling. Our floors were dirt with large mounds of sand. I slept soundly in those days and woke up early every morning excited about a new day of adventures with Maggie. The little hills and lush green landscape were paradise compared to my four years spent standing on hard cement in a barren cell.

I felt sad Frankie would never experience Maggie's home and see the sun and the sky again. I wished he could walk through life without steel bars. I imagined him bathing in the water for hours and then cake himself in mud from head to toe. I could see him graze all day long while enjoying the warm sun on his back. I could hear him trumpet as loud as he wanted—just being an elephant doing elephant things.

***

Miss Lacey visited Maggie and me about a dozen times the first six months I lived in paradise. She was a very sweet girl who brought us treats of pineapples. One time she brought us peanuts. Frankie had been right, the peanuts tasted awful. I spit them out of my mouth. Miss Lacey laughed. Maggie did not like the peanuts either and made a horrible face. I sucked some in my trunk and blew them out all over Miss Lacey. Maggie did the same. Miss Lacey got a big kick out of us. No more peanuts after that day. During the second six months she visited less than five times. As we both grew bigger, Mr. Howard, our caretaker, brought us extra hay several more times each day. He had kind eyes, dark-stained teeth, and wild hair. He cleaned our stalls every morning and made sure we had plenty of hay and water when he put us to bed each evening. Sometimes on warm spring days he would spray us with the hose. Maggie and I wondered if we were not part fish because of how much we loved the water. The second year I lived in paradise, we saw Miss Lacey only twice. She was growing into a lovely young woman and always as happy to see us as we were to see her. She seemed to enjoy our animated greetings of little squeals and trumpets of excitement.

One day in early spring, as Maggie and I fed on the tender green grass, Mr. Howard showed up with two men we had never seen before. They stood near the barn and watched us for some time. I felt like I was back at the prison. I had always hated being watched in my prison cell. These men made me feel uncomfortable. Frankie loathed being stared at in prison. He would stand in his prison cell and stare blankly at the visitors most of the time. When in a really bad mood he would turn his back on the crowd. I always followed what Frankie did. During these times he would again talk about life with his family. He still missed them terribly after all those years. Of course I offered no comfort to him because talking about his family made me miss my mother. Sometimes I missed her so much I physically ached. I know Frankie shared the same ache but his had been dulled by the passage of time.

Maggie did not like the men watching us either and decided we should go for a walk. As we walked, she confessed, "Ernest, you've made me happier than

I have ever been in my life. I was so lonely when Miss Lacey went off to boarding school and stopped coming around as often. I hated being by myself day after day. I'm so happy you came here to live with me. I want us to be friends forever!" She batted her long beautiful eyelashes and hugged me with her trunk.

I finally admitted to her, "Maggie, you make my heart smile." I could tell she liked what I said because she batted her long eyelashes at me.

She then murmured, "I've grown quite fond of you, Ernest. You have become a very handsome elephant!" How I loved her at that moment.

We stripped bark off some trees and contemplated whether or not it was too cold for our first spring mud-bath. I remembered how beautiful she looked to me the first time I saw her sweet face two years earlier. She was even more beautiful that day. Still very petite, Maggie had no idea how adorable she was. In two years I had grown to more than twice the size of her. The sun felt deliciously warm on our backs even though the air was still cool. We looked at each other and both jumped into the pond at exactly the same time. Now *that* was a splash! The cold water shocked our bodies yet it felt good to wallow in the warm mud and shower each other with the cold water. We did not know it then, but that would be the last time we experienced the joy of playing together in the pond.

***

FOR THREE DAYS after our romp in the pond, it rained nonstop. We became bored from being stuck in the barn most of the day. On the second day, Maggie and I went out in the rain for a bit and splashed and trampled through the puddles with great glee and then ran back to the shelter of the barn when we became chilled. It was early spring and some days remained cool. We feasted on the fresh green grass the morning of the third day and watched as a strange truck coming toward our pasture got stuck in the mud. Two men jumped out of the truck and began to kick the tires and yell at the truck. This went on for quite some time as Maggie and I stood in the rain and watched in amusement. When the men eventually released the truck from the mud, Miss Lacey's dad appeared and the three men headed toward us.

Miss Lacey's dad brought us several apples which we devoured instantly. He fed us one apple at a time as the two men put chains around our necks and ankles. Miss Lacey's dad led us to the truck. What did we know? He coaxed us into the truck with more apples and hooked our ankle chains to fasteners on the floor of the truck. The chains around our necks were fastened to rods attached to the ceiling of the truck. Bewildered, Maggie placed her trunk in his hand. He patted her kindly and would not look at her face. Miss Lacey's dad gave us a few more apples. He would not look me in the eye when he said how sorry he was. Sorry for what, we wondered?

3

ON THE ROAD

If you live to be a hundred, I want to live
to be a hundred minus one day
so I never have to live without you.
—A. A. MILNE

IT SEEMED WE were on the truck for days. Throughout the bumpy and wretched ride, we stood in our own excrement reminding me of the months at the prison following Frankie's death. Maggie cried for the entire ride. We were wet, cold, hungry, and tired. It was impossible to sleep. Only once, when the truck stopped, did we receive water from two filthy buckets. I was so thirsty I drank all of mine and wanted more. Maggie looked at her bucket and trumpeted her distaste. She refused to drink. One of the men shoveled our dung into the bucket from which I had just finished drinking. Then the door of the truck slammed shut again.

The ride from then on was not as bumpy or as long. I tried to comfort Maggie to no avail. She thrashed in her chains and rubbed her left ankle raw. It seemed to take about another day to arrive at our destination. The two men released us from the truck and led us rather roughly to an enclosure—if you could call it that. My first glimpse revealed a tented roof and a cement floor, some foul smelling straw strewn about, and several adult elephants chained to large stakes in the ground. Maggie and I were chained to the same stake by one of our back legs and our front legs were chained together about two feet apart. We stood there snorting in shock and fear.

"Where are we?" Maggie gasped horrified. She began to tremble.

"Welcome to elephant hell," one of the elephants emitted a low rumble.

"Where are we?" I repeated for Maggie.

"We are in elephant hell. Who are you?"

"My name is Ernest and this is my friend Maggie."

"Well hello there. I'm Mary. I am weary after a long day. Let us get acquainted in the morning. I am sure you two need your rest."

Maggie who had not stopped crying since we left our home days ago wept quietly.

***

THE NEXT MORNING our legs ached from standing. We slept fitfully. Unfamiliar sounds filled the night.

Maggie's body was warm yet she shivered like she was cold. We both hurt all over and we were unable to lie down due to the constraints of the chains. I reached for Maggie with my trunk to comfort her but she was so hot I had to pull away. She let out a low moan. We stood there, hungry, bewildered, and exhausted.

We heard her before we saw her. A woman named Ms. Hope hummed and brought us our morning hay and water. At least the water was clean and fresh. Maggie finished her bucket in no time. She looked up for more. Ms. Hope filled her bucket from the hose and smiled at Maggie who finished her second bucket before the rest of us finished our first. "Thirsty little girl, aren't we, love?" Ms. Hope cooed. We received generous portions of hay and Maggie and I ate greedily. Ms. Hope, a kind soul who must have known how hungry we were gave us some extra hay and made us, "promise not to tell anyone." She refilled everyone's water buckets and shoveled and hosed out our areas. She threw some fresh straw all over the enclosure and as she was leaving blew us all kisses and promised to be back for our afternoon baths.

Maggie's condition seemed slightly improved after some hydration and food. I caressed her face with my trunk and she fluttered her beautiful eyelashes at me.

"Well aren't we a pair," snorted Mary. "How are we feeling this lovely morning in elephant hell?"

Mary looked to be middle-aged. I could tell she had once been a real beauty. The years had obviously treated her unkindly. Her eyes were dark and sunken and her skin hung loosely on her thin frame. She looked as if she needed to gain at least a thousand pounds. I saw a hint of who she used to be in her eyes. To look at her made me sad. One of her back legs was deformed.

There were three other adult females: Lilly and Rosemary, who were younger than Mary, and Eve, the oldest—who I later found out knew my mother. Mary trumpeted bitterly, "This place is the end of the line. No one gets out alive."

Maggie shuddered.

4

MARY

If people were superior to animals,
they'd take good care of them.
—BENJAMIN HOFF

MARY WAS GENERALLY good-natured, but had an edge to her. She got along well with the others and pretty much kept to herself. She was thirty-eight years old when I met her. Like Frankie, she had been taken from the wild and remembered her family very well. She was captured and shipped in a dark crate to an amusement park when she was five years old. She stayed there for only about six months with another young elephant.

"We didn't get along—or didn't *not* get along," Mary explained, "Her name was Sunny. We were so immersed in our own individual grief we didn't have the capacity to console one another. We couldn't bond. I felt terrible about it then and I still feel just awful about it now." She shook her head sadly.

Mary had then been shipped to a zoo where she joined the company of Bonnie, a teenager who immediately took to mothering her.

"She was so kind and tenderhearted. I loved her instantly!" Mary continued, "We became fast friends and spent almost five years together. She helped me to become whole again. Then Bonnie disappeared. One day she was there and the next day she was gone. During our morning bath, Bonnie was led out of the enclosure never to be seen again. I was lost and scared without her and fell into despondency once again."

At ten years of age Mary was sent to another zoo to be a companion to a young mother who had just lost her calf. "Mable was fifteen years old when we met. Her calf had been stillborn and she confided in me she was secretly happy her baby didn't survive. She existed at the zoo for ten years, three of them alone. She couldn't bear the thought of bringing a new life into a boring cement prison. We became great friends and remained together for ten years until Mable died of unknown causes." Mary sighed wistfully and rubbed her eye with her trunk.

Like Maggie and me, Mary had been brought by truck to elephant hell and had been there ever since. "I have spent eighteen years of my life in this hell. I have seen friends come and friends go. It is always devastating to lose a friend." Mary shook her head sadly. "A horrible place for elephants, this isn't living. We merely exist."

***

THE THING THAT struck me about Lilly and Rosemary was how they always rocked back and forth in unison. Their heads bobbed up and down nonstop. Fifteen years earlier they had arrived together from a small traveling show that went out of business due to the hefty fines placed on it for not treating its animals well. When I met them, Rosemary was twenty-eight and Lilly was thirty. They had been in elephant hell for seven years. Both were very pretty and not emaciated like Mary. Rosemary could have put on a few hundred pounds and Lilly, the smallest of the four, looked pretty well fed. Rosemary, who had been captured from the wild when she was almost three, remembered her family. She missed them very much when she allowed herself to think about them. Lilly, born in captivity like Maggie and me had no memory of her mother. She had been taken from her before she was a year old and bought and sold from zoo to zoo for eight years before being sold to the small traveling show.

The only time I saw Rosemary and Lilly not rocking was when they ate or slept. Rosemary always slept standing up while Lilly lay down underneath her. Sometimes they would bob their large heads from side to side or up and down nonstop even when they visited with the rest of us. I did not know it then, but they were anxious and scared out of their minds. I know now they coped the best they could.

***

EVE IS A chapter all to herself. I do not know what I would have done without her during the years I spent in elephant hell. I bonded with her instantly. I loved to gaze into her soulful eyes. Wise beyond her years and a repository of knowledge, most of what I know today I learned from Eve. She was thirty-nine years old when I met her and not beautiful. Something about her made me want to constantly be in her company. Maggie adored her and having never been around adult elephants, she immediately designated Eve as her long-lost mother. Lilly and Rosemary got a kick out of sweet Maggie and even Mary took a shine to her. Who could resist my beautiful Maggie?

5

TRAINING

*People speak sometimes about the bestial
cruelty of man, but that is terribly unjust
and offensive to beasts, no animal
could ever be so cruel as a man,
so artfully, so artistically cruel.*
—FYODOR DOSTOYEVSKY

MAGGIE AND I new to the world of performing had a rude awakening. We began the training regime our second morning in elephant hell. After Ms. Hope fed and watered us then cleaned our areas, we were introduced to two other humans. Mr. Arnold was a large man who commanded awe. About forty with a hard mouth and a condescending manner, he had an edge to him, his voice deep and gruff. Behind his black T-shirt was a great bulge of muscles, a body of massive strength, and a body capable of enormous power, a cruel body.

Ms. Charlotte, a mean-spirited, hateful human being had a permanent harsh scowl on her face as if she hated living. She always stood with her legs apart and knees locked, arms folded. Defiant, her eyes flashed restlessly. Eve taught me to always find the good in everybody. I never could find any good in Ms. Charlotte or Mr. Arnold. I remembered Frankie's words about the ways of humans and how some did not deserve to be in the company of elephants. I wondered if Frankie had ever met anyone like Ms. Charlotte or Mr. Arnold. Given the once-over from head to toe by both of them, Maggie shuddered. The hairs on her back stood straight up. She did not like these humans either. Maggie and I were led to an enclosed area with mounds of dirt and no grass. Our back legs were quickly tied together and we were shoved to the ground. Our front legs then tied together and we were beaten all over our bodies by means of a large stick with a sharp metal hook on its end. It seemed to last forever. Maggie's sobs pierced my soul. I was too horrified to utter a peep. Ms. Charlotte said she wanted us to know "who was boss." We were then left by ourselves, tied up, with no food or water and bleeding from our injuries. Maggie cried pitifully. My back faced her so I could not see her sweet face. I wanted to console her and could not. I was too shocked to speak. My thoughts floated to Frankie and to my mother. Had my mother experienced this so-called breaking in? I remembered how Frankie, *the dangerous elephant,* was beaten for days. How I longed to be able to talk to Frankie at that moment. My mind drifted to swimming with Maggie and the beautiful lush meadow we had played in just a few days earlier. The bright warm sun blanketed my body and I eventually fell into a deep sleep.

***

I AWOKE FROM my deep sleep to the sound of Maggie's moans. Finally able to find my voice, I rumbled a greeting. More heart-wrenching sobs. When I opened my eyes, Mr. Arnold stood over me, his massive frame blocking the bright sun. With a cruel sneer he untied my legs and prodded me to stand up. I do not know how long I had slept but once standing I realized how ravenous I was. I looked toward Maggie who was standing, her face tear-stained and her eyes swollen. Bloody welts covered her little body. Oh, how much I loved her that moment and would have done anything to protect and comfort her, yet I was powerless to do so. I rumbled and she rumbled back. I held her gaze and she mine as we scarcely breathed in anticipation of what might happen next.

Surprisingly, nothing happened. They led us back to the enclosure with the others. Mary gently kissed Maggie's face, then mine. Eve quietly rumbled a greeting. Rosemary and Lilly rocked in unison.

Mary was the first to speak. "Humans use fear and pain to get us to obey them," she snorted bitterly. "They think they have to tear us down psychologically to teach us tricks. They aren't satisfied until they break our spirits." She flapped her ears in indignation.

"What kind of tricks?" I asked, remembering Frankie had chosen not to perform any.

"Can you stand on your head?" Mary asked.

"Stand on my head?"

"For starters, can you sit up like a dog? Can you defecate on command?"

Maggie, still in tears, snorted her own indignation.

Mary continued, "We are chained and food is withheld for punishment. Shipped around like a piece of rented furniture, we never know where we will end up!"

Maggie bellowed in horror.

"We have no autonomy. We don't get to chose when we eat, drink, or sleep. At the whim of whoever owns us, we are chained for hours and days on end in freezing temperatures or suffocating heat. And for what? We belong in the wild with our families and friends." Mary's ears flapped wildly and she stomped her front foot for emphasis.

"Just to be an elephant and do elephant things," I added wistfully, thinking of Frankie in his cement prison for ten-plus years. How had he managed, I wondered?

Sweet Maggie trumpeted, "Stand on my head? No way!"

"Stand on your head or get the crap beat out of you, literally," rumbled Mary who stomped her foot again.

Rosemary and Lilly continued to sway in unison, eyes dull.

Mary continued, "When I was young, I went through this same painful breaking in. It doesn't stop until we totally surrender. Usually takes about a week. Except for the strong willed elephants, who refuse to succumb and unfortunately drag out the torture. The humans will win. They use fear, pain, hunger, and thirst until we stop resisting and totally submit. The sooner you two stop resisting the better. You need to accept your fate!"

"Why?" I asked dumbfounded as I sucked my trunk.

"Because they will ruin you if you don't," Mary and Eve answered in unison.

I did not understand. Frankie and I would have done anything for Mr. William. All he had to do was ask.

Mary told us she had seen many animals ruined from cruel treatment. She explained, "The pointy stick is called a bull hook, or ankus. The humans use it as a tool to punish and control us. The handle is made of wood or metal and at one end there is a sharp steel hook. Both ends cause pain. The humans apply pressure with the hook to the sensitive spots on our bodies which causes us to move away from the source of pain. Humans think our skin is tough but it is so sensitive we can feel pain from an insect bite. Our most delicate and sensitive areas are around our mouth and eyes, inside our ears, and at our anus. A bull hook is an easy way for the humans to inflict pain and injury on our tender skin."

I roared to the ladies, "Ms. Charlotte and Mr. Arnold actually beat us with the handle!" I was so mad tears streamed down my face.

Maggie sobbed violently, terrified. Eve and I gently wrapped our trunks around her tiny, ravaged body. Mary gently patted Maggie's face with her trunk. Rosemary and Lilly rocked back and forth staring at Maggie. Entranced and frozen in a hypnotic state as if the whole thing were surreal.

We heard her before we saw her. It seemed Ms. Hope *always* sang to herself when she watered and fed us and cleaned our enclosure. Maggie and I gulped down our hay, consuming every piece before it hit the ground. Our water buckets were sucked dry before Ms. Hope finished filling the others' buckets. Ms. Hope, extra tender with Maggie and me, must have known how raw and fragile we were. She coaxed us out of the shelter and gently washed the blood off our bodies. I winced as the water stung my sores and Maggie quietly wept during her bath. Mary and Eve affectionately tended to me and Maggie. They rumbled softly and kissed our faces with their trunks. How I loved them that awful day.

***

THE BEATINGS CONTINUED for another week, each one far worse than the previous. No words can describe the daily dread we experienced. The overwhelming terror caused us to shake with fear. My own pain seemed like nothing compared to the sound of Maggie's screams as the hook repeatedly hit, prodded, and poked her body. The memory of my mother and Frankie occupied my mind during the beatings. I thought of happy days with Maggie in paradise. Between her screams, I rumbled to her to think of the pond, the mud-wallows, and playing in the rain.

Overnight our lives became a dangerous place with humans a threat to our safety and well-being. Maggie and I never saw the world the same way again. No safety in our world. No mercy. Eve and Mary's love and support helped heal our beat-up souls when we returned to the enclosure each day. They tenderly touched our wounds with their trunks and gently kissed our faces. Very quietly they helped us every single day, despite their own misery. They taught Maggie and me to always be kind and to keep our hearts open in the presence of suffering because when one of us suffers, we all suffer. Lilly and Rosemary rocked back and forth.

Ms. Hope took to Maggie more than me. She sat on the ground in our enclosure with Maggie's head on her lap and sang to her. She gently rubbed the top of her trunk between her eyes. After Maggie fell into a fitful sleep, Ms. Hope sat with her for hours. Maybe she wanted Maggie to know not all humans were bad. She wanted us to know some humans genuinely loved us and cared about our well-being. It seemed Maggie always brought out the best in everyone she met. All of us helped Maggie survive her breaking in. But she would never be the same Maggie. Sometimes when I looked into her eyes, a vacant stare looked back at me. She had checked out and was not there. Other times when her eyes met mine my heart burst with joy to see my sweet Maggie looking back at me. But these moments became less and less frequent as time went on.

It was difficult for Maggie to understand why we became the targets of such violent cruelty. Maggie loved everybody, and everybody loved Maggie. She tried to please Ms. Charlotte by performing all her tricks on command as well as anticipating what she wanted. No matter how well Maggie performed and did as Ms. Charlotte commanded, there was no relief from the tirades. Maggie did not know how to be angry, even when Ms. Charlotte acted downright hateful toward all of us. It was not in her nature. I always wondered what made Ms. Charlotte so mean. She was the most mean-spirited human I have ever personally encountered. Our fear of her and Mr. Arnold and their power over our lives became as real as breathing every day.

Each of us coped in whatever way we could. Mary made fun of Ms. Charlotte. We communicated among ourselves through rumbles too low-pitched for the humans to hear. With Ms. Charlotte on her daily rampage, Mary would crack a joke or pull a prank. Several times she took Ms. Charlotte's hat off without her noticing and threw it out in the parking lot. Ms. Charlotte always found it later, very dirty and very smooshed. She would then lash out at the nearest elephant and whack one of us with her awful hook. Another time Mary untied Ms. Charlotte's apron and all her stuff fell out onto the floor. Rosemary and Lilly weaved back and forth uncontrollably and neurotically. Whenever we heard Ms. Charlotte or Mr. Arnold approaching, Lilly and Rosemary defecated in fear. Eve and Mary's hairs would stand up on the back of their necks. I always knew when Maggie felt anxious because she would grab my trunk with hers whenever she was aware of Ms. Charlotte's pending presence.

Even when we did everything right, Ms. Charlotte berated us. She cruelly swung her sharp hook and randomly struck one of us for no reason. With a contemptuous sneer she seemed to enjoy our cries of pain. I believe that is what changed Maggie, the unfairness of it all. There was no way to anticipate what would happen next. We lived in constant fear of being hit for no reason. Sometimes when we anticipated we would be hit, we were not. It felt as if we were the brunt of some cruel joke. I remember the day Maggie realized this was her life and there was nothing she could do about it. That was the day I saw her heart break in two. We did as well as we could with our situation. As time went on, instead of being scared to death all the time, we became mentally detached like Eve. We watched ourselves and our surroundings from a bird's-eye view, like it was all happening to someone else. It was the only way we could survive

Maggie and I stayed on the road with Eve, Mary, Lilly, and Rosemary for two years. Performing was stressful with the constant glare of the bright lights, the head-splitting music, the din of the crowds' cheers and whistles. In between shows, humans shuffled past. No one stayed for long. By the time Maggie and I arrived in elephant hell, our new friends had already seen millions of nondescript human faces, every day, in dozens and dozens of different cities, year after year after year.

We were always very tender with one another, yet that part of my life felt as cold and uninhabitable as the moon. What always baffled me was the way we were treated as evil beasts. Mary resisted a command before the last performance one night. Tired and irritable, she could not do what was asked of her. Ms. Charlotte yanked her away from us. When we returned to the enclosure after the performance hours later, she was a bloody mess. All four legs were chained to keep her incapacitated. Maggie burst into tears and Eve moved a bucket of water toward Mary who voraciously sucked the bucket dry. It was a terrible way to live and we remained afraid. Standing on balls or on our heads made no sense to us, but if we resisted we were beaten severely. We desperately wanted to live unafraid. Our days were filled with fear, stress, and profound cruelty. The pain and suffering we were forced to endure week after week, month after month, year after year is still incomprehensible to me. We became a family and were always there for each other. I lived through this and yet it still seems as though it happened to someone else. Rosemary had untreated sores on her feet that would never go away and her joints ached. Sometimes she and Lilly cried for no apparent reason, tears pouring out of their eyes. Weary to the bone, my two comrades obsessively rocked back and forth day after day after day.

Mary—the largest, though gaunt from years of having food withheld—still loomed tall over all of us. It was heartbreaking to see her in such a horrible state. Ms. Hope showed up after the parking lot emptied of all the spectators to clean Mary's wounds and gave her some bananas which she devoured. She brought a truck load of hay for the rest of us. Mary never flinched as Ms. Hope tended to her. Eve stayed within trunk distance of Mary who remained quiet. After Ms. Hope left for the night, I asked why we all did not just run away.

"There is no contest!" Mary growled and flapped her ears vehemently. "Humans may be small next to us elephants but they have all the power. Elephants who dare to fight back are hung, electrocuted, or shot dead. They are the lucky ones. I wish I was dead! How did we get so unlucky?" A flood of tears streamed down Mary's sad face.

"Where would we go?" snorted Eve.

"Anywhere is better than here," Mary rumbled through her tears.

"Let me tell you a story." Eve sighed, waving her trunk passionately.

"After my initial breaking in, I went to a traveling show with five other elephants. At five years old I was the youngest and obviously terrified out of my mind. Beatrice, the oldest, took a shine to me. The kindest, most gentle elephant I have ever known, she understood my situation as she had been there herself many years before. How I adored her! The other four were also a good lot. We all experienced the rigor of the training regime before coming into the possession of Mr. Atticus, a decent man who took excellent care of us. He dearly loved us all. He never hit any of us, ever! Beatrice starred in his show for twenty-three years. She was in her late thirties when I arrived and the obvious matriarch of the group. Hannah, Isabelle, and Florence were all younger, and Beatrice's son Benjamin, a gangly teenager had the longest legs I have ever seen on an elephant! On the road with Mr. Atticus for nine months of the year, we stayed in two towns a month. The downside was the train rides between towns, the boxcars suffocating, especially in the summer. I remember being so hot and miserable I thought I would die. At least we had three months off during the winter when we rested and foraged to our heart's content. Mr. Atticus kept us watered and well fed while on the road, and it wasn't a horrible life, though far from ideal.

"Beatrice and all the others were captured from the wild when very young and remembered their families just as I did. We spent hours, days, and years talking about our families and life in the wild before being incarcerated for reasons we could not understand. We were a close-knit, very bonded group and we helped each other through our emotional ups and downs. After five years, one of the performers became ill, and Mr. Atticus brought in a last-minute replacement named Mr. Scott.

"Something about him made Beatrice uneasy. He seemed afraid of her. For whatever reason, Beatrice did not like Mr. Scott. She didn't trust something about him. Two days later Mr. Scott and Beatrice were dead."

We all gasped, waiting for Eve to continue.

"The most horrible part of Beatrice's death is she died because she wanted to eat a piece of watermelon."

"Watermelon?" Maggie squeaked, sucking her trunk in disbelief.

Eve continued softly. "Mr. Scott, obviously an unskilled and uneducated nincompoop who was ignorant to the ways of elephants, was put in charge of us. The day after he was hired, he rode Beatrice with a bull hook in his hand. He led us single file to a water hole where we could drink and hang out before ShowTime. Half a watermelon lay near the side of the road, and Beatrice turned to eat it. All of us elephants loved fruit, and Mr. Atticus kept plenty on hand, but none of us loved watermelon the way Beatrice did. Mr. Scott prodded her with the bull hook to keep her walking. Wanting the fruit, Beatrice ignored him and walked toward it. In his inexperience and frustration, he hit her hard in the side of the head. Now, remember, Mr. Atticus had never hit any of us with anything. Ever! Well, Beatrice wrapped her trunk around stupid Mr. Scott's waist, hurled him off her back and he slammed violently into a wooden kiosk. Then she calmly walked over to where Mr. Scott hit the ground, set her foot on top of his head, and squashed it. She then ate the piece of watermelon."

Again, we all gasped, this time in horror.

"Surprisingly, later in the evening, we all—Beatrice included—performed and everything went fine. However, as word spread, the humans of the surrounding towns where several performances were scheduled demanded Beatrice be destroyed or the show be canceled. Mr. Atticus—completely devastated, since it was clearly not Beatrice's fault—felt responsible for allowing an inexperienced human to handle his cherished elephants. The only way Mr. Atticus would be able to perform was if he showed up without Beatrice.

"The day after Beatrice killed Mr. Scott, she did not perform in the evening show. Instead, Mr. Atticus left her chained outside the railroad cars. Of course, he planned to come back and get her after completing the evening show. Mr. Atticus left her enough food and water to last until he returned several hours later.

"Some troublemakers in the town wanted Beatrice to pay for her bad behavior. Several humans decided to take matters into their own hands and came around to the railroad station. They put a chain around Beatrice's neck and attached the chain to a loading crane. Apparently, the first time they lifted her struggling into the air the chain broke. And when the chain broke, she fell to the ground with a horrible thud and broke her hip.

"That was how we found her when we returned later after our last evening performance. Mr. Atticus decided to cancel subsequent shows because the performance did not go well without Beatrice."

We listened in stunned silence as Eve continued the story of her greatly loved Beatrice. Eve took a deep breath and fought back the tears. "When it became obvious we did not to want to leave her, the humans from the town felt it appropriate for the rest of us elephants to witness Beatrice's murder so we wouldn't get any ideas about doing the same. Mr. Atticus insisted we be led away to a watering hole before Beatrice was killed. As he was outnumbered, we stayed put, right beside the crane. She lay on her side, her hip badly broken. I could feel her terror and saw the confusion in her eyes. Her pain was palpable. She reached her trunk toward us as we drew near. I will never forget the look of bewilderment and horror on her face as her eyes met mine. We extended our trunks in comfort. A larger chain was placed around her neck while several men held Mr. Atticus refusing to let him go. They hoisted her again and her life ended a few minutes later. We watched in horror while our adored friend thrashed in pain, confusion, and terror, then took her last breath. We trumpeted our revulsion and indignation loudly as Mr. Atticus led us away, our squeals and roars of rage deafening. Her death destroyed Mr. Atticus. He yelled, 'Murderers, bloody murderers!' as he fought back tears. I'm not sure who was the more stunned— Mr. Atticus or us. They burned her body on a pile of railroad timbers. We could smell her burning flesh, unable to get the scent out of our trunks for weeks afterward." Eve paused as she shuddered from the memory.

"Poor Beatrice," she continued. I can't imagine what she was thinking the last few seconds before her life ended. Later we all stood huddled together in the darkness to try to stop ourselves from shivering from the fear."

"Mr. Atticus, dejected, never went on the road again after returning to our winter home. We tried to be a comfort to Benjamin, completely withdrawn after the death of his mother. His head hung low, his trunk dragging on the ground. I didn't see him eat for at least a month. He grew gaunt. Mr. Atticus tried to maintain us. But after almost two years, he lacked the funds to feed us all the way we needed to be fed, and had to sell us off. Hannah, Isabelle, and Florence went to three different zoos. Mr. Atticus would not allow any of us to perform on the road again, horrified about what happened to his beloved Beatrice. The good-byes were heart wrenching each time one of us was led tearfully away.

"I never saw any of them again. Late one afternoon, Benjamin lay down for a nap. He never got up. He was twenty-two years old. I believe he died from a broken heart."

Eve closed her eyes and shuddered at the memory. We all reached out to her with our trunks. She opened her eyes and sighed.

Maggie took Eve's tearful story especially hard and cried her own tears as well. "What happened to you? Weren't you lonely after all your friends died or left? How old were you?"

"I was a little older than you are now, Maggie."

"Almost ten?"

"Yes, at almost twelve years old, the only one left to be sold, I stayed with Mr. Atticus for almost a year after Benjamin's death. I adored him and he clearly adored me, but I felt lonesome for my own kind. I think he sensed it and he spent a lot of time talking to me and keeping me company. He created a small mud-bath for me to wallow in providing me some happy times. With a healthy appetite and five acres to forage to my heart's content, I almost doubled in size from when we first came off the road!"

"How did you end up in this awful place?"

"The same way we all did," Lilly squeaked, pitifully bobbing her head. "Bought and sold like possessions. We are not possessions, and do not belong to the humans. We belong in the wild!

"We elephants are very intelligent. And very unlucky," Lilly continued bitterly. "When I think of all the underfed elephants I have met, the beatings, being chained for long hours, the 'accidents,' I always ask myself, why don't we react? Well, sometimes we do. The humans know we could break our chains anytime we want, but we don't. And you know why?" she asked in a shrill trumpet. "The reason we don't is because we know to escape would only mean being gunned down or hung like Beatrice. Lots of older elephants have seen this happen many times and they pass it on to the younger ones. I know the elephants who finally lose it and go on a rampage, like Rosemary's son Jackson, made a conscious decision to commit suicide. And no one can tell me any different!"

She was so passionate and articulate I hardly believed it was Lilly, who almost never spoke as she tirelessly rocked back and forth.

"And the so-called accidents?" She continued even more shrilly. "Ever notice how only the humans who abuse us are killed in all the confusion? Think about it. We have no natural enemies in the wild. We swim in the rivers, we play in the mud, and we love our families and friends. We live our lives not wanting to hurt anyone. We choose our victims for good reasons. Remember, an elephant never forgets! We never forget the cruelty and suffering of our family and friends at the hands of ignorant humans!"

Lilly's rocking became epic. Rosemary hobbled over to her and they weaved and bobbed in unison as tears rolled down Lilly's sad face. She was inconsolable.

"Let me continue for Lilly," Rosemary chirped. She had a sing-songy way of speaking.

"My son Jackson was taken from me when he was a baby around two years old. He remained confined in a concrete room and beaten repeatedly with a sharp bull hook! He cried out in pain. It was beyond horrible to hear his screams of pain as he cried out for me. I was powerless to come to his rescue. When he returned to me, he showed me where they struck him in his most sensitive areas: behind his ears, on top of his toes, in back of his knees, and around his anus. I told him not to resist, the humans wanted to hurt and scare him in order to break his spirit so he would be obedient. I was angry at myself for being helpless to do anything." Her sad eyes flashed angrily and she hung her head.

"Bewildered and angry, he spent most of his time in chains, along with the rest of us, doing nothing. His little bones ached from lack of exercise. His diet was monotonous and he stood in filth and excrement, deprived of every aspect of normal elephant life. Beside ourselves with boredom, we all were miserable—Jackson especially. He couldn't understand why this was happening to him. He wanted to be a baby elephant and play baby elephant games.

"Before a show one afternoon my sweet Jackson playfully head-butted one of the humans, who beat him in public to the point he screamed in terror and begged not to be hit. The human claimed to be 'disciplining' him. Jackson just wanted to play. This went on day after day, week after week, year after year. Jackson was lively and high-spirited and no matter how cruel the beatings, they never broke his spirit. The beatings angered him and he took the cruelty very personal. At five years old he couldn't take it anymore and he tried to escape during a traveling performance. He didn't make it. Three months later he tried to escape again. Again he was unsuccessful, and he paid a very high price.

"The next year we performed on the road, existing in the usual barren concrete-floored tents in various parking lots and chained between shows, while the beatings continued. Jackson vacillated between pain, indignation, anger, boredom, and despair. Still very mischievous and playful, he always pulled the older elephants' tails. He just wanted to be an elephant and do elephant things!

"The summer of the following year, Jackson snapped. After performing on the road for nearly four years, he grew tired of being beaten, whipped, and kicked. The pain and the boredom of confinement were more than he could bear. He wanted to be free. He resented the bad treatment and become angry and aggressive. He was finally hurt enough to hurt back. In hindsight, I should have seen it coming. He had become more restless and agitated than usual. He went absolutely berserk during an afternoon show. He stomped a human to death who was about to strike him with a bull hook. He then mangled another with his tusks. And let me tell you, they both deserved what they got. He finally escaped from the area and took off running. I only hope he enjoyed his freedom as he roamed through the streets on his stubby short legs and trumpeted his little head off for more than an hour. The local police killed him with forty-seven rifle shots. *Forty-seven rifle shots!* It took him over an hour to die. He died a horrible and agonizing death, only six years old. Afterward, the humans put his bloodied little round body into a dumpster like a piece of garbage!"

We all were stunned. Poor Rosemary, her eyes filled with tears as she rocked in unison with Lilly and sobbed. "Rest in peace my sweet little one, your suffering is over."

How could my cherished friends go through such unfathomable cruelty and so many horrifying situations with such amazing fortitude? I could not imagine the grace it took, being torn between spending the rest of their lives in chains and beaten every day for no reason, or trying to escape, knowing they might be brought back and punished even worse, or ultimately shot! And yet they were always there for one another, no matter what. I loved them more than words could ever say.

***

Maggie and I were lucky to have Eve and Mary with us while on the road. The cramped boxcars were stifling hot in the summer and bone chilling in the winter. They taught us to poke our trunks out through the slats at the top of the boxcar for air or else we would have suffocated to death. Mile by torturous, dull mile, the heat oppressive and smothering, there were no words to describe our misery. The harsh heat made the boxcar airless. Eve taught me how to breathe shallowly to keep calm and not panic. One oppressively hot day, I became so panic-stricken I could not catch my breath. Eve stayed right by my side and breathed with me. Her calming influence helped me to breathe easier. Most times we stood in our own excrement for days without water. I thought I would pass out from the stench. During those times

I often thought of Frankie and of my mother; it was much too hot to even talk. Sometimes when I enjoyed pleasant memories of them an overwhelming emptiness consumed me and the tears flooded like a dam released. The ache of missing my mother and Frankie became physically unbearable at times, and I reeled from the onslaught of their memories for days. I thought about Frankie and how much he missed his family, and wondered how he managed all those years. Then it would be over and I would be fine until the next time.

During the winters, with no hair to speak of, no blankets, nor heat, we traveled exposed to the full harshness of the cold, huddled together to keep warm. Our breath hovered in the air between us.

Mary flapped her ears angrily. "I can't believe the indignities we endure! Elephants aren't made to withstand the cold. We do not have the extra layer of fat under our skin needed for such extreme temperatures. We are not polar bears! I cannot feel my feet, they are so numb from the cold!"

She was right. Many a day and night during those seemingly endless train rides I could not feel my feet due to the cold. As the nights grew steadily colder, the wind blew hard through the slats of the boxcar and caused our teeth to chatter loudly, making sleep impossible. Eve and Mary protectively insulated Maggie and me between their generous bodies, while Lilly and Rosemary rocked and swayed, listless and miserable, their eyes totally dead.

Whatever forces were at work remained well beyond our control and stretched the limits of our endurance. Nausea, headaches, anxiety, and fear became the norm of our everyday life. I learned to expect them, learned to live with them. Sleep deprived, no exercise, unrelenting noise, no peace. Even water was withheld so we would not urinate during a performance. Each new place smelled the same: popcorn, dung, cotton candy, sweat, cigarettes, and diesel fuel. Day after day we performed our tricks dutifully and without enthusiasm. Our lives so depressing, sometimes we barely recognized ourselves. Our powerlessness was debilitating.

***

MOST OF THE time on the road, Mary, Eve, and I talked about our families and friends. Maggie felt left out because she had no memory of her family. Her only elephant friend had been me until we ended up in elephant hell. Mary and Eve loved to share their stories of life in the wild. Rosemary and Lilly rocked in unison, eyes lifeless. I wondered if they heard us or, if they were a million miles away, where did they go?

Mary had a sister ten years her senior and two brothers, one five years older than her sister and the other five years older than Mary. She remembered some hyenas stalked her family herd one night when she was very young.

"My mother let out a growl that terrified me and I ran under her body and hugged her leg with my trunk," she said. "My two aunts, three cousins, my grandmother who was the matriarch, and my mom's younger brother along with my sister and two brothers formed a circle around my mother and me. I remember being terrified as my grandmother, with her ears spread wide, charged at the hyenas. I could see everything happening from underneath my mom. One of my aunts flanked my grandmother, her ears spread wide as well. A formidable force not to be reckoned with, the hyenas began to back away! My grandmother and aunt trumpeted loudly and charged the hyenas, who then went scrambling!"

Maggie and I listened wide-eyed. I thought about Frankie and his wild family and wondered if Mary's family knew Frankie's. Mary and Eve laughed; their sad wrinkly eyes sparkled as they remembered a different life far away and a long time ago. They loved their families and their lives. They loved doing elephant things.

Mary took a deep breath and exhaled a long heavy sigh. "My cousins and I wallowed and romped in the mud most days. My brothers wrestled, and I watched, always within trunk distance of my mother. We used the mud to protect our skin from sunburn and insects."

I remembered Frankie telling me about the wonders of mud for elephant skin. Deeply annoyed there was no mud to bathe in at the prison, he hated the mosquitoes biting his sensitive skin.

As if she read my mind, Eve rumbled wistfully, "There are no mud-baths in this hellhole. My skin is ruined from years of lack of mud!"

Mary nodded. "I look decades older than my years! This place has not been good for my skin either. And I come from a long line of real beauties!"

True, Mary appeared to be a lot older than her years. One had only to look at her to know she had been horribly neglected and abused. She looked worn out. We became silent, each lost in our own thoughts and memories as Lilly and Rosemary ceaselessly rocked back and forth.

6

Eve

*The elephant is the beast which sur-
passes all others in wit and mind.*
—Aristotle

In the still night air, the moon glowed brightly in the cloudless sky. The others, fast asleep, snored loudly after a long grueling day. I found myself wide awake after my second night of performing. As I listened to the unusually loud chirping of the crickets, I noticed Eve staring at me in a funny way from across the enclosure. "Why are you looking at me like that?" I whispered feeling uneasy.

"I recognized you as soon as I saw you." Eve smiled sweetly at me. "You favor your mother with your stumpy legs and big dark eyes. Except for the tusks, you are a duplicate version of her."

"You knew her! What happened to my mother?" I bellowed loudly then sucked my trunk anxiously. "I miss her every single day. Even when I am not thinking about her, I miss her."

"Well, let me start at the beginning." Eve let out a long heavy sigh. "After I left Mr. Atticus, I went to a zoo that housed two other elephants. I was a little older than you at the time, almost thirteen. I met your mother, who was a little younger than me, and an older elephant who became a surrogate mother to your mom and later to me. After losing Beatrice, I hungered for the comfort of an older, wiser mother figure. Your mother and I became fast friends. Not a whole lot to do at the zoo, but we made the best of it."

"What was her name?"

"Her mother named her Suay, which means "beautiful". She was renamed Clementine by the humans after her capture and I always knew her as Clementine."

Clementine. I liked the sound of that. Clementine. Clementine. I said her name over and over to myself.

"The older elephant Maria was in her late twenties and your mom had just turned seven. And what a dark-eyed beauty! The most beautiful of all of us, she drew crowds from miles around. Maria and I were tall elephants due to our long legs. Your mother had the shortest legs I have ever seen on an elephant until you! We called her Stubbs." The gray skin around Eve's eyes crinkled as she smiled at the memory.

"Maria, who was captive born, gave birth to a still-born little boy when she was very young—too young, in my opinion. Your mother, who was wild born, came to the zoo when she was five. Of course, she and Maria bonded immediately. And what a pair they were! Gracious and kind, they welcomed me immediately. Maria always said, 'There is plenty of love to go around.' We passed the days eating lots of hay and bananas. More than enough food, yet the ground stayed hard, so there was no loose dirt for dust-bathing and no mud for wallowing. Clementine constantly pulled Maria's and my tails, then stole our bananas. My first summer, I became so sunburned I couldn't lie down, it hurt so badly. There was no relief from the hot sun. Later in the fall, a new human named Ms. Sue noticed our discomfort and put up an awning for us. What a relief! We loved her immediately. She paid attention to us and always tried to make our lives better, just like Ms. Hope. She hosed us off three times a day during hot weather and, let me tell you, it stayed hot for some time. We were thankful. She hid snacks all over our enclosure for fun and gave us some old tires to play with.

"After several years, Maria started complaining about her feet and legs hurting."

Oh no! I thought as I remembered Frankie.

Eve, with a faraway look in her eyes, slowly flapped her ears as she went back in time. "Clementine and I enjoyed kicking the tire around the enclosure, and one afternoon while we played, Maria collapsed. We immediately ran over to her. She couldn't get up."

Just like Frankie, I remembered wistfully.

"Your mom and I trumpeted our distress loudly. We hugged her with our trunks in between bellows of anguish and fear of losing her. She couldn't get up. We tried to help her to her feet but her legs didn't have the strength to hold her up. When Ms. Sue arrived, she immediately called in the veterinarian. They stayed with her for several hours while Clementine and I nervously hovered nearby. We rumbled our concern to Maria, who rumbled back, 'I will always love you two. Please don't be afraid for me. I have enjoyed every minute of our time together, my sweet precious girls. Always remember to be kind to one another. I have loved hearing your stories about your families. Please keep the wild alive by telling the younger ones your stories of what it means to be an elephant and how we ought to be living. Let them know this man-made illusion of elephant life doesn't even remotely resemble our lives in the wild.'

"We trumpeted our denial loudly. Then she was gone, thirty-six years old. We ran over to her and rubbed our trunks all over her body. Ms. Sue cried for a long time, and we hugged her all over with our trunks to comfort her. Maria's body was hoisted out of the enclosure and taken away within hours of her death. A long dark night for your mother and me, we cried inconsolably until the sun came up. We were still crying when Ms. Sue brought us our morning meal.

"Your mom was fifteen and I was twenty-four. We stayed at the zoo for about ten more years. Your mother"—the gray skin around Eve's eyes crinkled as she smiled at the memory—"was always too smart for her own good. A few years after Maria's death, a very handsome bull came to the zoo. He was housed in a separate enclosure and your mom could see him and smell him. She was smitten. He was a real looker. And huge! We looked like miniature elephants compared to him, especially your mom. His name was Henry."

Eve flapped her ears, looked me right in the eye, and smiled mischievously as she continued, "One rainy afternoon your mother went from our enclosure into Henry's enclosure. I never did figure out how she did it. Ready to mate, she really wanted your father. Ms. Sue was beside herself, concerned Henry would hurt your mom since he was literally twice her size. Your mother would have nothing to do with her. She never left your father's side for over a week. She came back to our enclosure when she was good and ready. Twenty-one and a half months later, you were born. It was an extremely emotional day for your mother. We helped you stand as your wobbly little legs slid out from under your 287 pounds on the slippery cement floor. When Ms. Sue arrived in the morning, you already stood on your own and suckled your little heart out. Your mother beamed with pride for you! Ms. Sue brought your dad around to see you. Imagine he and your mom with trunks entwined, gazing at you. Your dad held you with his trunk, and was then led away by Ms. Sue. The next day he was gone. We never knew what happened to him. Ms. Sue disappeared too. We figured she went with your father, though I can't be sure. All we knew is one day they were with us and the next day they were gone.

"Not long afterward, you, your mother, and I moved to a much larger open area. We still maintained the same sleeping area, but the ground seemed not as hard and we had a lot more room to walk around. Two other female elephants were already there when we arrived. They had just come off the road and retired to the zoo, middle-aged and very haggard looking like our Mary. Yet they were so sweet, the kindest old ladies. Marguerite and Isabelle lived on the road together their whole lives. As soon as we showed up, they were all over you. They chirped and squeaked and ran their trunks all over your little body. Your mother beamed. You were constantly surrounded by us. We loved you, Ernest. You were priceless. We became fast friends and enjoyed getting to know all about each other as one lazy day melted into the next.

"The only problem was our new human. He was extremely heavy-handed, and your mother did not like being poked and prodded by him. And she very definitely did not want him anywhere near you. She was very protective. Marguerite and Isabelle told us the story of how Mr. Carl—I think that was his name— beat an elephant senseless with a bull hook one day. Afterward, she became just a shell of an elephant. Her soul had been stomped out. She obeyed every command and did her tricks perfectly, like a robot. Your mother did not like him and was extremely afraid of him. We all were.

"When you were about nine months old, he separated you, your mother, and me from Isabelle and Marguerite. Out of sight of each other, we communicated through low-frequency rumbles. They were close by, so we kept in touch. They wanted daily updates on you.

"When you were almost three years old, some men came to take you away from your mom. She put up a tremendous fight. We tried to protect you from the men who beat us with sharp hooks. You were sedated with a dart gun. When you went down and the men came toward you, your mother broke her chains loose from the wall, all her motherly instincts in full force. She was ready to fight to her death. The men hit her hard with their hooks and then sedated her. She went down hard. I watched in horror as your mother lay on the ground out cold, and you—with your legs tied, wrapped in a large blanket—were dragged to a truck. And then you were gone.

"When she came to, she fretfully looked for you for days. Hysterical, she trumpeted your name, her huge heart breaking in two, beside herself with grief. After a few days, her head hung low, her tail listless, she stopped eating. She refused to obey Mr. Carl's commands. He beat her upside her head mercilessly with an ax handle while all four of her legs were chained together. She just stood there and took the onslaughts. A terrible coward, Mr. Carl felt he was a big man by beating a chained elephant. This went on for weeks. It was horrible to watch, and I was powerless to do anything to help her. She never flinched once. After losing you, she lost her will to live."

"My poor mother," I choked back tears and sadly hung my head.

"Unchained in the yard for our twice-weekly baths and monthly inspection by the vet, your mother had become thin and very frail after she stopped eating for almost a month. Mr. Carl raised his arm with bull hook in hand to strike Isabelle for no apparent reason. Your mother grabbed him with her trunk and hurled him in the air. Dead as soon as his body slammed to the ground. She embraced Isabelle's face, trumpeted loudly and fled. I never saw her again after that day. We heard she was shot dead in the street. Someone else heard she went to a research lab that studied aberrant elephant behavior. The irony is there was nothing aberrant about her behavior; she behaved as any brokenhearted mother elephant would. She hated Mr. Carl and his abuse. All I know is something inside her died the day they took you from her. I believe she felt she had nothing to live for. You were her pride and joy and there was never a prouder mother. I know your mom was crazy about your dad, too. He became known as the biggest bull in all the land!"

I looked up at the bright, starlit night. I wondered how many stories those stars could tell. "My poor, sweet mother. Clementine, wherever you are, I hope you know you are loved and adored and sorely missed. I am so sorry you fell into the wrong hands." I wondered what became of my dad.

Eve's ears flapped and she gently touched my face with her trunk to comfort me. "Ernest, please know she loved you with everything she had. Her huge heart broke in two the day she lost you. She deeply missed you and was still grief-stricken the last time I saw her."

Lost in our private thoughts about my mother, we remained silent for a while. Eve broke the silence and continued, "Within a month, our group split up. I ended up here in elephant hell with Mary, Lilly, and Rosemary. I never saw Marguerite or Isabelle again. Kind gentle souls, I hope they ended up in good hands. They would be in their late fifties or early sixties if they're still alive."

I could not help but think we were fellow travelers in a world gone awry. We had found ourselves in an unrecognizable place eons away from our natural surroundings and everything familiar, like a bad dream from which we could not wake up.

***

AFTER A LONG, hot, thirsty, and frustrating day, Eve and I, beyond exhaustion, stayed up another night and chatted into the wee hours of the morning. The others, bone tired and long asleep, snored loudly. We were too tired to sleep.

"What is this thing, memory?" I asked her as she munched on some hay, her weariness obvious from three performances in one day. "And where do our friends and family go after they leave us for good?"

"Maybe they are alive somewhere because we remember them," she answered thoughtfully.

"What do you mean?"

"If we did not remember them, wouldn't they cease to exist? We exist because we see ourselves and others exist because we see them."

"If no one sees us, would we not be invisible and therefore not exist?" I rumbled, flapping my ears thoughtfully.

"But we *can* see ourselves." Eve's ears flapped and her eyes sparkled knowingly, "We are aware of ourselves!"

I told her about Frankie and how I constantly missed him. "It is a dull ache, always there, some days worse than others. I think about him even when I am not thinking about him."

"Just because we can't see the stars on a cloudy night doesn't mean they aren't there. The same is true of our loved ones. Just because we can no longer see them doesn't mean they aren't here," she rumbled matter-of-factly. "Frankie exists because you remember him. He lives inside of you. Your memory allows you to feel him, smell him, and see him. His love endures forever inside you." She hung her head low, and her trunk fell to the ground. "Think of Rosemary's son Jackson. Rosemary keeps him alive in her memory. He lives inside her. Because of her memory, he will stay young forever. His sparkly eyes, short stumpy legs, handsome face, little round body, unbreakable spirit, his constant head-butts. That is how we will always remember him. He is alive in us. He left this world before the humans beat his pride out of him and killed his spirit. Perhaps he is one of the lucky ones," she rumbled softly.

7

Elephant Down

The wild, cruel animal is not behind the bars of a cage. He is in front of it.
—Alex Munthe

Maggie and I had been on the road almost two years. We slept hard one night, exhausted from four performances in one day. A little before dawn, Rosemary collapsed in our cement enclosure. The thud from her fall woke us all. Maggie and I wanted to offer comfort, but because of our chains we could not reach her. Eve and Mary, within touching distance, hovered near her protectively until Ms. Hope arrived three hours later for our morning feeding and baths. Lilly, rocking even more than usual bellowed her anguish as Ms. Hope unchained her and then the rest of us. Needless to say, none of us felt like eating our morning meal. Rosemary suffered from arthritis so severe in her hips and knees she could not lie down for fear of being unable to get up again. Every night for years she had stood guard over Lilly while she slept. Now Lilly stood guard over her trusted friend. Ms. Hope sat down and cradled Rosemary's huge head on her lap. Rosemary died two hours later. I hoped she did not feel afraid as she took her last breath.

Ms. Hope was crestfallen. We all were. I immediately thought of Frankie who had fallen and could not get up. I wondered if Rosemary chose to die or not. Finally free from the fear, punishment, deprivation, and boredom, her eyes stared vacantly at nothing. She was only thirty years old and slightly older than Frankie when he died. Lilly was bereft and bellowed in anguish. Mary and Eve stood quietly nearby stroking Rosemary's limp body with their trunks. I hugged Maggie to comfort her as she reached for me with her trunk. We witnessed unbearable and intense grief.

That was exactly how Ms. Charlotte found us when she arrived at noon.

***

WHAT HAPPENED NEXT remains unclear because it all happened so fast. None of us remembered exactly how it happened. This is the best I remember it.

In her usual raging fashion, Ms. Charlotte, with arms flailing, hit Eve and Maggie hard with her bull hook and screamed, "What in the world is going on in here? Why aren't these elephants fed and watered?

There is dung all over the place! Ms. Hope, get up before I get you up myself!" Ms. Hope did not budge.

"Why you lazy, no good…" Ms. Charlotte raised her arm with hook in hand to strike Ms. Hope, who was still on the ground with Rosemary's head on her lap. Mary very quickly positioned herself between Ms. Hope and Ms. Charlotte causing the back of her leg to receive the full force of Ms. Charlotte's rage from the pointed end of the bull hook. Mary cried out in agony and fell to her knees under the impact of the blow meant for Ms. Hope. Ms. Charlotte raised her arm to again strike Mary, but Eve knocked her down with her trunk, which sent the bull hook flying. Enraged, Ms. Charlotte stood up and charged straight toward Eve as Lilly swung around wildly and, with her ears flapping and trunk swinging, blocked Ms. Charlotte's path. By this time Mary rose unsteadily back to her feet. Ms. Hope could not get out from under Rosemary's dead weight. Maggie, paralyzed with fear, clung to me with her trunk. By this time Mr. Arnold arrived to see what all the commotion was about. Ms. Charlotte stood up again and screamed in anger, "Kill the beasts, kill them all!" Lilly spun around and with her trunk knocked Mr. Arnold down, but not before taking a bloody hit in the face from the full force of his bull hook. Mary, still unsteady on her feet, fell sideways onto Mr. Arnold, and in the commotion Ms. Charlotte got trampled until unrecognizable. Blood everywhere—both human and elephant.

Eve and Lilly helped Mary to her feet. Ms. Hope cried softly and gently rocked Rosemary's head. We stood in stunned silence for a very long time. None of us knew what to do next. We stared helplessly at each other, our powerlessness palpable.

***

FINALLY ABLE TO get out from under Rosemary's large head, Ms. Hope checked on Lilly's and Mary's wounds. She hosed us all off and disappeared for a while as we stood around feeling helpless. She returned with some men I did not recognize who took Ms. Charlotte and Mr. Arnold's bodies away. She then hosed out our enclosure and brought us all some fresh hay. Unexpectedly very hungry, I devoured mine and most of Maggie's who was so upset she could barely swallow. Eve and Mary chewed silently, lost in their own thoughts. Lilly stood protectively over Rosemary while Ms. Hope gently rubbed some ointment on her and Mary's gaping wounds. Mary reinjured her bad leg during her fall onto Mr. Arnold and could not put any weight on it. Ms. Hope disappeared again and soon returned with a veterinarian. Mary's leg was broken. The veterinarian splinted it and gave her something for the pain.

Ms. Hope was the first to break our eerie silence. "I don't know what will happen to all of you. But anything will be better than this dreadful place. So many times I've wanted to quit, but I couldn't leave you here alone without any compassion or kindness. Not all humans are like Ms. Charlotte and Mr. Arnold and I am deeply sorry you were unlucky enough to have fallen into their hands. I am relieved they are gone and can no longer, ever, harm another animal."

Maggie put her trunk in Ms. Hope's hand to comfort her. "Ah, my sweet Maggie, you have endured the most horrible of circumstances in your young life and yet you are still as sweet as ever!" Maggie squeaked loudly and hugged her with her trunk. Eve and Mary trumpeted in agreement. I walked over to them and they both hugged me with their trunks before we tried to console Lilly and pay our respects to Rosemary one last time.

Rosemary lay where she died for days; Lilly never left her side. Finally, after three days she was hoisted onto a dilapidated old truck. Her head hung off the back of it and her trunk dragged on the ground as the truck slowly drove her away. Now, I am no expert on death and dying, but after the life she endured, it seemed beyond disrespectful to be carted off like a piece of garbage. She was only thirty years old! None of us said it out loud, but I guarantee the shudders we experienced as the truck drove away that day, were the result of each of our own horrible thoughts of what would happen to her body.

***

EXHAUSTION SWEPT OVER me, yet I could not sleep. Maggie slept soundly next to me, her trunk draped over my body as she snored softly. I could not get the picture of Rosemary being carted away out of my mind. I missed Frankie terribly at that moment.

Badly shaken after witnessing the death of our friend, we stayed unchained in the enclosure for about a month, with Ms. Hope taking care of us each day. She somehow found us fresh hay and bananas every day! Of course, I thought of Frankie as I savored every delicious bite. I could see his smiling face as I too smiled.

Eve laughed, "Why do you smile as you eat?"

"I was thinking of my friend Frankie, who loved bananas more than anything. The only times I ever saw him smile were when he ate bananas or when he talked about his family."

Eve looked deep into my eyes and smiled that knowing smile of hers as she slowly chewed her own bunch of bananas with great relish.

***

EVERY MORNING AFTER breakfast, and then again after our afternoon feeding, Ms. Hope took us out for a brisk five-mile walk across a barren field near our enclosure. It felt so good to walk. My legs ached when we finished, but I did not care. Lilly and Eve skipped along like two young elephants, much to the amusement of Maggie and me.

"These legs were meant for walking!" they would trumpet in unison, then interlace their trunks. "Not standing in one place like a tree trunk!" they roared between bouts of laughter as they merrily enjoyed being able to stretch their legs. They tossed twigs in the air and kicked two discarded soda cans between them. Giggling like rowdy children, their faces beamed with childlike innocence and it was the first time I ever saw Lilly smile. A sense of well-being and lightheartedness never felt before filled our days.

Mary, unable to join us, eagerly welcomed us back every day with loud trumpets as if we had been away on a very long journey.

During our second month in Ms. Hope's care, several humans came to look us over. Maggie rumbled anxiously and grabbed my trunk with hers.

They reminded us of the humans staring at us when we lived in paradise. I could tell Eve and Mary were nervous. Lilly, now solo, began her neurotic rocking whenever in the presence of strange humans. We had no idea what would happen to us, where we would end up, or in whose hands. During the third month Lilly was taken away in a truck by two sinister-looking men. They made us all nervous. They seemed to like Lilly's rocking; they thought she was dancing and decided to call her "the dancing elephant." They were too ignorant to know she was terrified and anxious with nowhere to run.

Lilly tried to appear brave as they loaded her on the back of an open truck. As it drove away, she turned toward us, made eye contact with Eve, and rumbled, "Good-bye my friend. I will never forget you." As Eve fought back tears, Maggie and I tenderly hugged her with our trunks to comfort her. Her head drooped. "Lilly was such a sweet girl who was badly traumatized from all the abusive treatment," she sighed. "Her nerves sandpapered raw, she went mad, causing her to constantly rock. At least she had Rosemary for comfort. Now, without Rosemary, I can't imagine her loneliness and terror if she falls into the wrong hands." Eve hung her head and cried silently.

Maggie and I did not leave her side until Ms. Hope returned with our evening meal.

I do not know what kind of life Lilly lived after she left us that day. I never saw her again. I can only hope she experienced some sort of compassion and kindness along the way.

***

SEVERAL WEEKS LATER, after our morning walk, Hope, Maggie, Eve, and I returned to our enclosure and saw Mary lying down on her side. I wondered why in the world she would be sleeping at that time of day. Two unfamiliar humans stood over her. Eve rumbled from deep within as Ms. Hope sprinted over to the men. Eve's rumble scared Maggie and me, and we clung to each other with our trunks. We could not hear what they were saying, but Ms. Hope was obviously agitated. As we got closer, I heard Ms. Hope screaming, "Murderers, you bloody murderers!" She then became so distraught she could not talk. Eve stopped dead in her tracks. Maggie and I followed suit.

"Please say it isn't so," Eve rumbled.

Maggie and I thought Mary asleep and did not understand what was happening. We wanted to wake her up and let her know we were back from our walk, as we looked forward to her spirited welcomes every day when we returned. But something in the way Eve rumbled made us stay put. We looked at each other and relocked our trunks. Something was not right.

"Please say it isn't so," Eve rumbled, much louder this time.

Ms. Hope, hysterically crying and with arms flailing, yelled incoherently at the men. They just looked at her and shook their heads as they walked away.

Eve bolted over to Mary and frantically inspected her with her trunk. Maggie and I came up right behind her as Eve trumpeted the loudest most anguished trumpet I had ever heard. In fact, I am not so sure her trumpet could not be heard around the world. Maggie let go of me and burst into tears. Then it hit me.

A little confused and a lot scared, I squeaked out a barely audible, "What happened?"

"She was euthanized," Eve roared her indignation, ears flapping wildly.

"Euthanized?"

"Put to sleep."

"Put to sleep?"

"They killed her!"

"Why?" I stared at Mary's body not comprehending.

By now Ms. Hope was hugging Mary's trunk and Eve straddled Mary's body while Maggie gently touched her face.

I was having a hard time comprehending Mary was gone. We had joked around during breakfast earlier that morning. She kept stealing my bananas as I pulled her tail and danced circles around her! I now gazed at her thin frame and once beautiful face; she looked as though she were sleeping peacefully. It took me a little while to realize just how peacefully.

"I do not understand."

Eve's sad, wrinkled eyes met mine. "Mary is too old to breed. Her deformed leg would keep her from going to any of the 'good' zoos. She would need a long time to heal a leg that has been broken many times. She can't go back on the road and perform. She has become a liability."

My mind swam, too confused to cry. "Oh," I rumbled softly and walked away from the scene. I wished Frankie was there. My heart stuck in my throat. In a little over two years I had made four new friends and lost three of them at the hands of humans. I wondered how many friends Mary had seen come and go. *Liability?* I did not know what that meant, but I could guess she had outlived her usefulness. The sun glared and a butterfly landed on the tip of my trunk as a cool breeze blew across my face. Just when I thought I had seen the worst human nature had to offer. I wondered what Mary's final thoughts were in the last few moments of her life. Did she understand what was happening to her? I hoped she was not afraid. The whole thing seemed disrespectful to me. I kicked a few rocks across the barren field, and then returned to pay my final respects. Rest in peace, sweet Mary, your suffering is over.

***

STILL REELING FROM Mary's death, Eve, Maggie, and I quietly enjoyed the warmth of the sun one breezy sunny day. It was one of those days neither hot nor cold, just between cool and warm, with a gentle breeze. I held my face toward the sun with my eyes closed.

"Caresses." Eve's soft rumble broke the silence.

"Caresses?" Maggie and I echoed simultaneously.

"The breeze is a gentle caress from those we love who are no longer with us. Today we are receiving lots of caresses."

"Who is caressing us?" Maggie demanded as she batted her beautiful eyelashes.

"Mary and Rosemary just caressed us. Did you not feel it?"

"How do you know it was them?" Maggie again demanded.

"Shhhhhh," Eve scolded softly. "When the world is very quiet, far from the noise of humans, and we are extremely still, our loved ones will gently comfort us; sometimes in the form of a breeze on a nice day like today; other times, a single star in the night sky, or a butterfly gently landing near us. All of these brief encounters are reminders our loved ones are still with us, even though we can't see them except in our memories. You must open your hearts, or the opportunity will be missed. It will never happen with noise. The noise is a barrier. Today is a particularly quiet day."

I immediately thought of Frankie and of my mom. "Mom, Frankie. Are you there?" I trumpeted. A small gust swept over us.

"Did you feel that?" Maggie squeaked, wide-eyed.

I looked at Eve, who smiled knowingly, then shut her eyes to enjoy her often missed loved ones.

8

TO BREED OR NOT TO BREED

Education of the mind without educat-
ing the heart is no education at all.
-ARISTOTLE

FOR THE NEXT several years, Eve, Maggie, and I, under the care of Ms. Hope, resided at a breeding facility.

"Breeding facility?" Eve snorted and flapped her ears indignantly. She was not the least bit interested in any of the males sniffing around.

According to Eve, Maggie and I would be too young to breed in the wild. I guess the humans were expecting me to mate with Maggie or Eve. At twelve years old, I had no idea about any of that stuff. So, for almost two years, we lived at a breeding facility and none of us ever bred. We were confined in a fairly large pen where at least the ground felt soft and we had plenty of food. And we could move around during the day! The water trough was always full, and all I can say is, a lot of water fights occurred among the three of us. Ms. Hope gently scolded us as she filled up the trough with water for the seventh or eighth time each day. At night we stayed chained in our enclosure, which, of course, we all hated. At least we could snuggle up together when we lay down at night, and this helped me to sleep soundly most nights. We were a lot better off than we had been in elephant hell, and Ms. Hope tended to us in her usual caring manner. We received fresh hay several times every day and we ate to our hearts' content. Maggie and Eve spent a lot of time together without me; "girl talk" they called it. I admit it hurt my feelings to be excluded. I think Maggie felt kind of bad for me, because she batted her beautiful eyelashes at me and hugged me with her trunk after particularly long sessions of "girl talk".

The thing that stands out most in my memory of the breeding center is the mosquitoes. We would try to dust-bathe as much as we could, but there was not a lot of loose dirt with which to accomplish this. Eve had the hardest time. For some reason the mosquitoes really liked to bite her, and she was miserable. Maggie and I were bitten a lot, but not as much as Eve. And did we ever itch! Eve taught us how to use sticks to scratch the places our trunks could not reach.

**

MAGGIE AND I were wrestling one morning after breakfast before Ms. Hope arrived to give us our daily baths.

We did not hear Ms. Hope's usual humming before she arrived, and Maggie noticed sooner than me she was crying. Eve tried to comfort her. Maggie scurried over to see what was wrong and I slowly made my way over to the girls. Eve, Maggie, and I exchanged worried glances as Ms. Hope sobbed hysterically. She could not talk; her entire body racked with tears. Maggie touched Ms. Hope's face with her trunk. I am not sure how long I stood there helplessly and watched, but everything that happened afterward seemed to be in slow motion and made up a scene I shall never forget as long as I live.

A truck with a large open bed came right up to our enclosure, and three men jumped out of the cab carrying chains and ropes. It all happened so fast, it seemed surreal. A rope went quickly around Maggie's neck, and another around her back legs, which were then tied together. They chained Eve to a stake in our enclosure, and as one of the men came toward me Maggie screamed and bellowed. The man talked to me, but I could not hear a word he said. I had to help Maggie. She screamed again as I saw a horrible bull hook grab a hunk of flesh from her left hip. She was hoisted onto the back of the truck by two of the men and all four of her legs were chained to the sides of the truck bed in five seconds flat. Her back was to me, so I ran to the side of the truck to see her beautiful face bewildered and scared as she began to cry. Eve roared and broke loose from the stake, chains still attached to her legs, her trumpets deafening, ears angrily spread wide. One of the men hit her in the face with the bull hook, causing her to cry out as she reeled from the pain. Another man hit me on the backside with his bull hook as I tried to reach for Maggie with my trunk. Eve stood right beside me, blood running down her face, and reached for Maggie. Somewhere sounding very far away I heard Ms. Hope screaming for the men to stop.

"Stop hitting my friends! Stop hitting my friends, you stupid fools! Stop!!!"

Surprisingly, they listened to her. For what seemed like a very long time, the earth stood still, without sound. "Let them say good-bye to their beloved friend, you idiots." She spoke softly and tearfully. The men moved away from us, and respectfully helped Ms. Hope onto the back of the truck, then stepped away and silently got in the cab of the truck while Ms. Hope tenderly rubbed the top of Maggie's head.

Eve, Maggie, and I hysterically hugged each other with our trunks. The lump in my throat constricted my ability to breathe, let alone say anything. Maggie sobbed so violently her stomach heaved, making it difficult to communicate. Ms. Hope managed to eke out a few words. "Good-bye my friends, I will never forget you." Beautiful Maggie kissed Eve's bloody tear-stained face all over, and then embraced me as she held my eyes with hers. I hung on to her even after the truck began to pull away. I ran beside the truck until I could not keep up. Her beautiful eyes never left mine until she and the truck became smaller and smaller and disappeared completely from my sight.

***

THE WALK BACK to the enclosure remains the longest and loneliest of my life. I remember it being hard to breathe. Not because I was out of breath, it was the lump in my throat. I felt sick. When I came back into view, Eve walked slowly toward me. We met and continued to walk in silence— —back to what, I wondered. Side by side, we plodded back to no Maggie and no Ms. Hope. There were no words.

A young man we never saw before was cleaning out the enclosure when we returned. The trough overflowed with water and there was plenty of fresh hay waiting for us. He took one look at Eve and immediately washed her off with a hose. "What did you do to yourself, my sweet?" He fussed as he gently washed her face. Her left eye swollen shut from being hit. He was not Ms. Hope, but he meant well and we really appreciated his kindness. His name was Mr. Skipper and he was younger than Ms. Hope. He seemed genuinely concerned about Eve and me. I could tell he knew we were hurting beyond our physical wounds. He cleaned us up and put some ointment on us and then hugged each of our trunks before he left. I never saw him again.

9

THE BIRDS AND THE BEES

I want to run
I want to hide
I want to tear down the walls
That hold me inside
I want to reach out
And touch the flame
Where the streets have no name
—U2

THE DAY AFTER Maggie's departure, and almost three years at the breeding facility, Eve and I moved to a zoo. An uneventful move, the zoo must have been near the breeding facility because the ride in the truck went quickly. I had grown quite large, my tusks now considered dangerous weapons. Not a great zoo, but definitely a step up from the cement prison where I had resided with Frankie. I was the only male elephant among several older females. The floor was hard packed dirt, not much better than cement. And we had room to move around some, not enough for long walks, but we could move. There was no vegetation or mud to play in, but we did have a canopy for shade. We were never out of view of the curious humans all day, and when out of view, our legs were chained at night. Every night we remained chained almost twice as long as we were unchained during the day.

From the time I arrived at the breeding facility through the first few years at the zoo, I went through a growth spurt during which I again more than doubled in size. I became taller and stockier than all the females—including Eve, who was not petite. I still continue to grow today, just not as fast as an adult. Eve told me I would continue to grow in height and weight my entire life.

When I was sixteen, I experienced my first phase of sexual aggression. I thought I was losing my mind. All I could think about was mounting not one, but all of the females in our enclosure. The glands on my face became swollen and they secreted constantly. I peed all over myself and I could not stop rumbling. I could not eat; I could not sleep. The others basically ignored me, causing the already increased levels of testosterone surging through my body to make me even more aggressive. I wanted to knock down walls and break out of the enclosure. I badly bruised my shoulder when I actually tried to knock down a cement wall. I limped for weeks afterward! It is a madness I still endure, though at the time I had no idea what was happening to me. I actually attempted to mount Eve! Needless to say, she put me in my place. We were soon separated after that little episode. I remembered Frankie telling me how his uncle and older brothers had left the family herd when they reached puberty. Later, when I calmed down and was back to my normal self, Eve enlightened me. This time we conversed over the cement wall of our now separate enclosures.

"When you become taller and larger than all the adult females, your mating stage has begun," Eve explained. This allows you to successfully mount a female."

"Oh," I rumbled embarrassed.

"Older males are usually more successful with mating anyway. You should reach your sexual peak when you are between forty and fifty-five if you live long enough. You can still mate in your sixties—like my grandfather, who in his sixties was still going as strong as any forty-year-old."

I remembered Frankie telling me about his father being quite the "older stud." He impregnated many females due to his long life. He was sixty-three years old the last time Frankie saw him. Frankie was his twentieth offspring!

Eve, being the repository of knowledge she was, continued, "Males need size, strength, and experience in order to mate. Younger males aren't usually as successful for several reasons. Mounting is a skill that requires experience. My grandmother told me that females prefer older males and frequently refuse to stand still for the younger ones. Penis size can hinder a younger male's ability to successfully impregnate a female."

"Oh," I squeaked. Embarrassed, I touched my sixteen-year-old penis with my trunk.

Eve continued, "At sixteen, you weigh about half of what a forty-year-old would weigh. Larger, older males usually overpower the younger, smaller ones. A young male lucky enough to mount a female is usually forced off by a larger male or knocked off by the female!"

I hung my head and apologized to Eve.

"No matter," she gently rumbled. I hung my head and was glad she could not see my embarrassed face.

"Sounds complicated," I rumbled. "I do not remember Frankie going through any of this craziness during the nearly five years I spent with him. Can some of us avoid this phase?"

"My guess is that Frankie was depressed. Do you know if he was or not?"

As always, Eve was right on the mark. I had to smile wryly, "Yes, Eve. I remember he always ached for his family and could not wait until he saw them again!"

Eve sighed. "Well yes, depression, improper nutrition, loneliness, lack of exercise, can all cause our bodies to be out of whack. Captivity robs of us our elephantness!"

"How often will this happen to me?"

"It depends on your age. A surge of testosterone like what you just went through usually lasts a couple of days. The length will increase with age until you are about fifty. Then it will start to lessen."

I could not imagine going through this insanity for more than a day or two, which was bad enough.

Eve gently reached her trunk over the wall to touch me. "Males don't reach their sexual prime until they are around forty. Physical condition, body size, mass, and experience due to age allow older males to father more than half the offspring in an area. The longer you live, the more successful you will be at mating. If you are lucky and live to old age, you could father many. My grandfather, one of the largest and most well-known males in all the land for almost thirty years, died at sixty-six years old, right before I was captured. He fathered at least thirty others we knew of. Unfortunately, most males in captivity don't live long enough to become fathers."

"They die young, like Frankie." I rumbled, and wondered if I would ever be a father.

"In the wild," Eve continued, "male mating calls can carry more than two miles in the air and signal to other males to keep away. Males ready to mate are aggressive and dangerous. Humans can't hear these mating sounds. The female uses her own mating calls to broadcast her availability to males many miles away, also through sounds unable to be heard by humans. We can feel the vibrations to these calls with our sensitive feet."

"I wonder how many faraway females heard my calls the past couple days," I grunted. The other females were still ignoring me. It seemed they were not only uninterested in reproduction but uninterested in even discussing it.

"Things have become out of sync in captivity. Many of us are not even remotely interested in mating due to the stress of the traveling life or the boredom and lack of stimulation in prison—as you call it. Most of us do not want to bring new life into our captive environments. What kind of life is this?"

The more I heard about the wild, the more and more disillusioned I became with captivity. I wondered where my sweet Maggie had ended up and what she was doing. She would be thirteen. Was she close enough to hear my rumbles? Would she know it was me? I wondered if she ended up in good hands. Had she mated? Was she a mother yet? And my mother; whatever happened to her after she trampled the human? Had Maggie killed anyone?

I rumbled a powerful echoing sound, after which I lifted my head to listen for a response. I repeated this rumbling for several hours seeking to make contact with Maggie. There was no response.

Eve reached for me again over the wall. She always knew, the wisest elephant I have ever known.

I do not know what I would have done without her in those days. I was crazed with pain at the loss of Maggie, and sometimes when I thought of her and wondered where and how she was, the whole essence of her flooded my senses, as if she were right there at that moment, and I felt a tremendous sense of loss. I physically ached for her. Maggie reminded me of everything that was good in the world, and her absence left a huge empty place in my heart. As the days turned to weeks, and to months and years, the ache never went away, though it became duller. Like the ache I felt for Frankie and for my mother, it was always there. I often thought of Mary, Rosemary, and Lilly, but did not ache for them like my beloved Maggie. I missed them though, and always wondered whatever became of Lilly.

10

SOLITARY CONFINEMENT

*Lots of people talk to animals.... Not very
many listen though...that's the problem.*
—BENJAMIN HOFF

EVE AND I continued our daily visits over the cement
wall. Not a great life, but not a bad one either. I found
myself wanting to be alone more than ever before. Eve
said my behavior was normal for a male my age due
to the solitary lifestyle of males in the wild. "Though
they may form loose bachelor herds, they spend most
of their time alone. Sometimes they will visit their birth
family."

"Birth family," I snorted bitterly.

"We create our own families in captivity," Eve
explained, flapping her ears. "Though it can be difficult with all the moving around we do. In the wild, a

female stays with her family her entire life. As I said, even the males will periodically visit their birth family."

"Stay with them or deeply miss them their entire life," I rumbled, thinking of Frankie.

"The humans don't understand our need for love and companionship. They don't seem to understand us at all," she mused wistfully.

"Why do they think they have to dominate us with whips and hooks?"

"They are afraid because of our size."

"Well, we are elephants!" I laughed. "It is all so unnecessary. We are gentle creatures."

"Yes, we are." Eve bellowed loudly, completely out of character from her usual soft-spokenness. "And we must show the humans who and what we are."

"How?"

"By being ourselves as much as we can in this bleak environment. Look at all those luscious trees outside our enclosure almost within our reach. We could try to reach for those branches and eat the delicious leaves and strip the bark."

"Why do they not put trees within our reach?" I asked not understanding.

"They don't know or care. We are here for their entertainment, though it is difficult to be entertaining in this environment."

I thought of mud-wallowing with Maggie in paradise. Now, *that* was entertaining! Along with unlimited trees, and grass and water everywhere, I remembered water fights with Maggie and how we ran, played, swam, and sunbathed. "If the humans want to be entertained by us, they should watch us in our own environment," I rumbled, flapping my ears.

"I know, Ernest. I know."

***

As I CONTINUED my solitary existence, I often thought about Frankie. I wished he was with me, to see me growing up and getting big like him. He had been so massive and I knew I was catching up. Of course, at twenty-five years old he had not finished growing. But at twenty years old I knew I was getting pretty close to being as large as he. My tusks were already three feet long.

It would have been so much fun to mud-bathe and to explore the habitat with him. I passed the time for the next few years daydreaming about the two of us roaming the wild forests. And there were my daily visits with Eve. Once a day, the humans opened the top half of the barrier so I could see the females. It was impossible to get over the cement wall because elephants cannot jump as I came to know.

I continued to grow in size and stretched my trunk out to see how far I could reach. By now, having the longest trunk of all the elephants at the zoo, I could reach the branches of the fig trees. I would grab hold of a branch, twist it with my trunk, and enjoy the delicious leaves, bark, and fruit. I became quite adept at this and shared my abundant findings with Eve and the others. We savored every bite, and I remembered Frankie smiling as he ate his bananas. I too smiled as I chewed. Eve, of course, knew why I smiled, and would smile as she slowly chewed her leaves, fruit, and bark. We always devoured every last leaf and twig, not even a morsel left on the ground, so delicious was the taste. This went on for months before any of the humans realized what was happening. The trees became lopsided, giving us away, but we had left no other evidence.

Early one evening, after I snapped a branch off for Eve, one of the humans came out of nowhere and hit me upside the head with the pointy end of the dreaded bull hook. I dropped the branch and reached for another, only to be hit again, this time right between my legs. I roared as the pain brought me to my knees and I fell back onto the human. I did not realize I had done so until I eventually got back on my feet. Hearing my roar from the pain, Eve trumpeted her concern.

***

I AWOKE TO a pain in my groin and my head throbbed. It was dark and I could not move very well. I got my bearings and realized my back legs were chained together and my front right foot was chained to the steel bars. It was almost impossible to stand up, and I snorted my distress to Eve.

"Don't panic."

"What happened?" Everything was fuzzy and I felt a little woozy.

"You were tranquilized. The humans were all over you like beetles on dung!"

I remembered the pain in my groin. "Did he die?"

"Instantly; it would be difficult to survive being sat on by a five-and-a-half-ton elephant!"

My back was to her and I could not see her face, but I knew her eyes twinkled with her all-knowing smirk. "It was an accident," I said.

"I know."

"Now what—live the rest of my life in chains?"

"Don't know. Let's try to get you up. If you lie down too long, your organs will be crushed."

"How long have I been down?"

"Too long."

"Rock yourself, put all your weight on your left hip, and pull with your right front foot and push with your left front foot. You've got about two feet of chain between your back feet."

It took me three tries to get up. Eve hugged me with her trunk over the cement barrier. The chain on my front leg prevented me from reaching the branches and I now faced the back of my enclosure. "The humans do not want to know us as we are," I complained bitterly. "Do they not know we eat leaves, branches, fruit, and bark?"

"I know, Ernest, I know." Eve's trunk kissed the tears on my face.

Apparently the humans considered me dangerous and dared not come near me. Chained and unable to move, the monotony brought on desperation. I lost count of the days and the endless solitary hours sent my mind wandering. I imagined Frankie in the wild with his family. I imagined the soft sighs of the night winds and the sweet scent of succulent grass mixed with fresh dung. His shared dream seemed real to me. I imagined the sun warming his back, a full moonlit night with lots of stars, and the soft earth beneath his feet. Eventually, my mind sank into an abyss of nothingness. After six miserable months or so of listlessly standing in my own excrement, I had the most welcome surprise.

"Well hello, Ernest, my boy!" said a familiar voice from long ago. "I've been trying to locate you for years."

11

ANOTHER TRUCK RIDE

*If you smile at me, I will understand
'Cause that is something everybody every-
where does in the same language.*
—CROSBY, STILLS AND NASH

I KNEW HIS voice immediately, though I had recognized his scent a few seconds before he spoke. He came around to look me in the face. I trumpeted an emotional greeting. Sweet Mr. William, so good to see you my friend! I caressed his face with the tip of my trunk as he hugged the top of my trunk with both arms. Eve told me later all the humans watched in awe as Mr. William gently navigated under and around my massive body. He unhooked all my chains, and even though he knew I could crush him in an instant, he was not the least bit worried. He knew I would never harm him. He brought some bananas and bamboo stalks, which I inhaled instantly. As I chewed on some of the fresh hay Mr. William had given me, he hosed out my enclosure, all the while humming and repeating, "It's gonna be OK, Ernest, my boy, it's gonna be OK."

After I gulped down all my hay, Mr. William hosed me off. I have to admit I smelled pretty rank and a long overdue bath was exactly what I needed. Mr. William always knew what to do. I remembered how much he and Frankie loved each other. I wondered where he had been all these years. Eve stood nearby, checking on me. We locked eyes and she rumbled, "Mr. William?" She always knew. She repeated his words, "It's gonna be OK, Ernest, my boy, it's gonna be OK."

That evening, after Mr. William left, Eve and I visited for a while. She overheard the other keepers say I would be leaving in the morning. "Where I am going?" She did not know for sure, but she knew it had to be a better place than where we were. She sighed heavily. "I will miss you terribly Ernest, but you can't stay here, chained your entire life. Now that you are labeled a dangerous elephant, the humans will keep you chained, unable to move."

The thought of being chained for life sent shudders through my body. I had heard of other elephants who received this horrible fate. I could not imagine never being able to turn around or move for the rest of my life. Then it hit me. I would be without Eve. She reached over the wall and held my trunk with hers as she searched my face. "Ernest, in the wild, you would have been kicked out of the herd if you had not already left by now. It is the natural order of things. Though it makes me sad to see you go, it's for the best."

"I will miss you Eve, more than words can say." We stayed together until the sun came up, both of us lost in thought. Mr. William showed up early with breakfast and enough treats for all of us. I smiled as I ate my bananas, which made Eve smile as she ate hers. Mr. William looked at us and laughed heartily. "Frankie taught you well, my boy. I see you have passed on the tradition." He reached through the bars and rubbed the top of Eve's trunk. She loudly trumpeted her thanks.

After breakfast, he told me it was time to go. The other elephants were totally disinterested in my fate, probably because they had seen many males come and go, but Eve's eyes never left mine. Mr. William led me out of the back of my enclosure and I lost sight of her. We circled back, and as he walked me through the zoo, we stopped right in front of Eve's enclosure. She reached through the bars with her trunk and I stopped and quickly hugged hers with mine. Mr. William rubbed Eve's trunk again and we silently walked away. My heart was heavy, but Eve was right, it was the natural order of things. It took everything I had not to look back as Mr. William and I left the grounds forever.

***

MR. WILLIAM GENTLY led me into a huge truck with eighteen tires. After I was situated in a straw-filled stall, he gave me some fresh bamboo. He had a bunk over my stall and stayed with me the entire journey. He talked to me a lot along the way, and other times we quietly enjoyed each other's company. It must have taken several days, because we stopped three times to refill my water and clean out my stall. Two of the stops were at night, and one was in the daytime. When we finally reached our destination, it was early morning. As Mr. William tenderly led me out of the back of the truck, I saw the sun coming up over some mountains. Birds sang, and I heard the trumpets of nearby elephants. Where was I? My feet sank into the soft ground and for a moment I thought I was back in paradise where I first met Maggie. Ah, again that oh-so-familiar pang for Maggie. A few humans stood nearby, and as Mr. William led me around the side of the truck, I saw two distinct fenced-in areas. Looking out at me from behind one of the fences were five adult female elephants. Four of them trumpeted their greetings loudly and one stared at me intently. She looked vaguely familiar and watched my every move, yet I could not place her. On the other side of the fence were three males of various sizes and ages, much more aloof than the females as they sized me up. One of the males did not have any tusks, and I noticed only one of them had tusks larger than mine. What is this place? I wondered, and trumpeted a general greeting to all the observers. "It's gonna be OK, Ernest, my boy," Mr. William said as he rubbed my face, "it's gonna be OK." He walked me over to a third fenced-in area I had not noticed at first and led me in. "Welcome to Bachelor's Forest, Ernest, my boy! I trust you will be very happy here."

On one side the females and on the other the males. I suddenly felt very self-conscious as all eyes were on me as Mr. William hosed me off and gave me more bananas than I could eat. I scanned the area I found myself in. It was large enough for me to get out of view if I wanted to, which made me feel a little better. A small barn stood at the other end about an acre away. A full water trough stood near the female fence where all the ladies patiently waited for me to take a drink. The males had already left for their daily routines. It seemed they knew the ladies would have to get to know me first. After my bath, Mr. William left my area, but I could see him hovering nearby. I ate some of my bananas and wished Frankie was with me. I wondered how Eve was doing without me and thought about Maggie and me in paradise. I could not believe how good the soft ground felt beneath my feet. I raised my trunk to the sky and breathed in the fresh clean air. Another deep breath. Eve taught me to breathe shallowly when we were on the road to pro-tect my lungs from the smut and diesel fuel. By now the sun was shining brightly in the cloudless sky, its heat warming my face. The warmth felt good upon my back. I closed my eyes and took another deep breath and recognized a familiar scent. What was it? It left as quickly as it came. A gentle breeze washed over me. Frankie? I sized up the females as I slowly walked to the water trough. One was enormous. I had never seen a female elephant so big. She was very pretty in spite of a large healed-over gash across the top of her trunk, right below her eyes. There were two tall elderly females with long legs like Mary's. One more beautiful than the other, they both had kind eyes. They looked to be mother and daughter, or maybe sisters. Another, eating from a stockpile of bananas, watched me curiously as she chewed. The fifth elephant, the most beautiful of them all, had short stubby legs and a very round body. Her eyes were the darkest and saddest I had ever seen, yet they did not take away from her beauty. As I approached, she stared at me right in my face in a way that made me very uncomfortable. As I neared the fence, there were loud rumbles and shrill trumpets of greeting as if I was a long-lost friend or relative. She continued to stare at me, right into the depths of my soul. This made me so self-conscious I had to look away from her. As I extended my trunk into the water trough, a very familiar voice rumbled softly, "Ernest?"

12

CLEMENTINE

Look deep into nature, and then you
will understand everything better.
—ALBERT EINSTEIN

"MOM?" I SQUEAKED in disbelief. I knew instantly when I looked into her face. Her eyes filled with tears as I breathed in her scent. She smelled exactly as I remembered her, my memory had not betrayed me. Clementine, my beautiful mother, stood right in front me. My knees felt weak; the cacophony of the others' trumpets deafening. She gently touched my stunned face; my entire body was racked with tears. I could not get control of myself. She kissed my face as she herself cried. We hugged with trunks entwined. Time stood still. The seventeen years without my beautiful sweet mother disappeared, and I was three years old again. I continued to breathe in her essence.

The other females, who had maintained a respectful distance, could not stand it any longer and placed their trunks all over my body to welcome me to my new home.

I do not know how long my mother and I stayed in our wordless embrace. Every breath I took was of her, my mother, my beautiful mom. The others had left for their daily mud-baths, foraging, and socializing. When we let go of each other, I saw Mr. William in my periphery, watching us and crying like a fool. Ah, Mr. William, what a kind soul you are! Unable to speak, my mother caressed my face and softly rumbled my name over and over and over again.

***

SUAY, MY MOTHER'S given name, means "beautiful". She was true to her name, and it was hard to say who was more beautiful, my mother or Maggie. My mother had long eyelashes like Maggie's, but her ears were not as big nor her trunk as short. Her eyes, though sad, were kind and dark. I definitely had her stubby legs and round body. Not quite forty years old, she had lived at Bachelor's Forest for a few years. She retired from the road after an accident with a human. The accident being the human was drunk and took a steel pipe to her friend one too many times.

"After I stepped on the evil Mr. Carl's head, I was moved to a substandard zoo, where I existed for a little over two years," she told me. "The extremely gentle and kind humans knew I was labeled as a dangerous elephant, yet treated me kindly and with respect. The enclosure was small, the ground hard— no trees, no grass, and no mud-wallow. Not even a man-made pool! And was it ever hot! During the day, while on display for the humans, I could not go to the tented area where I was chained in the evenings. There must have been a shortage of food because they only fed me twice a day and I became very thin. There was nothing to do. At first I didn't mind. I just wanted to *be*. But after a few months, I began to lose my mind. I thought of you, Ernest, every single day, and sometimes of the friends I had made along the way. My family forever etched in my memory, I daydreamed about being back in the wild with them. I paced back and forth for hours each day. I thought I would scream if one more human threw peanuts my way! To this day, I hate peanuts!"

I laughed. "Why do humans think we like peanuts so much?"

"One of the humans, a young man named Mr. Skipper, genuinely cared about my welfare. After about six months, he showed up and brought me bananas every morning. A few bunches a day. He talked to me for hours on end. He ensured my water trough was always full of fresh water and one day brought in a plastic wading pool. Much too small for me, I would stand in it ankle deep, two feet at a time and shower myself with water. Mr. Skipper filled it up several times a day and hosed me off on particularly hot days. He seemed to be learning as he went."

Could it be the same Mr. Skipper? I wondered.

"Concerned about my weight loss, Mr. Skipper started bringing me more food. Soon I was eating four times a day plus my morning bananas. He started to bring me branches, hay, and bark daily. I couldn't believe my good luck. After about another six months, he brought me an old tire to play with. I wasn't sure what to do with it, so I carried it around when I wasn't eating. I started to nap several times during the day and began to fill out. I was still too thin, but at least my ribs weren't showing.

"About a year or so later, another elephant was added to the already-too-small enclosure. We didn't get along as both of us wanted to be the boss, and neither of us would back down. Plus, she tried to steal my food after she finished eating hers. Her name was Sylvia, a tiny elephant at only three tons fully grown. She had been grossly mistreated before arriving at the zoo, and Mr. Skipper loved her dearly. We tolerated each other and after a few months, I left the zoo and went to work on the road, where I spent the next twelve years."

I knew only too well the horrors my mother endured on the road. We shared our awful stories. She saw her best friend shot to death after she tried to run away. I told her about Jackson. We talked of the smell of fear we knew all too well. Her human handler had been unnecessarily heavy-handed. My mother had tried to protect a very young elephant from the wrath of a drunken human.

"He was the cutest little elephant. I could tell he missed his mom. His name was Hank. He was five years old, lonely, and scared to death, and in spite of it all remained extremely good-natured. We took a liking to each other immediately. I was still crazy with grief from losing you, and he was the sweetest little guy. He had already been through the rigors of training! He wasn't performing yet, but was part of the twenty-three-month tour so he could get used to being on the road. He hated the long train rides and the extreme temperatures and desperately wanted someone to play with. I played with him the best I could, but I was gone a lot during the performances. We were playing one evening with an old popcorn bucket. We tossed it in the air with our trunks, and the game was it could not touch the ground. As he squealed with delight, one of the humans came into our area, drunk out of his mind. He started swinging an old rusty steel pipe around and struck Hank across the shoulder on his right side. The blow was so unexpected it sent Hank reeling clear across the enclosure. As he roared in pain the human dealt him another blow right in the face. This time he screamed more from terror than pain. Either way, it is a sound I shall never forget as long as I live.

"Who does that to a helpless child, and one so adorable? As I barreled toward the drunk, he came at me full force. I don't need to tell you there was no contest between my four tons and his hundred and fifty or so pounds. He was so drunk when we collided, he fell to the ground and his head split open on the steel pipe. He never knew what hit him. Lucky for us, the steel pipe had Hank's blood on it. It wasn't a week before Hank and I arrived at Bachelor's Forest. We have been here a little over five years. I do hope you and Hank will become friends."

I felt a pang of jealousy. My mother had actually loved another in place of me! But then I had loved Eve as a mother. Not *instead of*, though, I had never stopped loving my mother. As I sheepishly glanced at her, it seemed she read my mind.

"Ernest, I never stopped loving you, and have pined for you every single day of my life. You have grown into such a handsome young bull, and I feel cheated out of all those years we have been apart. We are almost like strangers!"

I ran my trunk across her face to comfort her through the fence, and then said, out of nowhere, "I know Eve."

"Eve? Oh Ernest, tell me all about my wise and trusted friend Eve!"

13

ALL ABOUT EVE

*Without friends no one would choose to
live, though he had all other goods.*
—ARISTOTLE

I TOLD MY mother all about Eve and how I would not
have lived without her. Her wisdom, grace, and compassion kept me and everyone she knew going. I told
her about Maggie and how much I missed her, ached
for her. I told her all about Frankie, and cried when I
thought about how I would never see him again.

"You would have loved Frankie and Maggie."

"I am truly sorry I will never have the honor. And
my sweet Eve. How was Eve when you last saw
her?"

"Eve is Eve. She hated to see me go, but told me
it was the natural order of things in the wild and how
I would have been kicked out of the herd if I had not

already left. It has only been a few days since I saw her. I miss her, Mom."

"Me too, Ernest. She was right there with me the night you were born. And a tremendous help. I had no idea what I was doing."

"She told me about that night. She loves you and misses you."

We both were quiet for a long, long time, lost in our own thoughts. I wondered how Eve was doing. Of course she would be fine, she was always fine, even when she was not. There was no one like Eve. My thoughts drifted to Maggie. I wished she could have been there to meet my mother. *My mother!* I could not believe how much comfort I felt that day just to breathe in the scent of her.

"Mom, you smell like you. Exactly like I remembered, I could recognize you without eyes."

"I knew it was you when your first foot stepped out of the truck and I couldn't believe my eyes. I thought I was dreaming. You look exactly the same as the last time I saw you—only a much larger version."

She smiled a sad smile and caressed my face.

"Back to Eve. How does she look, Ernest? Is her health good?"

"She looks tired, like all of us. Her spirits are OK and she seems healthy to me. The zoo where we were was not great, but we were fed twice a day."

"Elephants should be able to forage all day long! Two meals a day is unnatural!" She trumpeted her indignation and flapped her ears.

"There is nothing natural about the world we find ourselves in."

"Ernest, this place is as good as it gets in captivity. The humans pretty much leave us alone. We can stay out all night and sleep under the stars if we wish. Sometimes the nights get a little cool and we have a heated barn to sleep in or just to go in to warm up. The humans are here to help. That Mr. William is something else!"

"I knew Mr. William from before when he took care of me and Frankie at the zoo. His heart broke when Frankie died. Mr. William disappeared immediately afterward and I have always wondered what happened to him."

"Well," my mother sighed, "Mr. William started this place, probably right after Frankie's death. How long ago did he die?"

"A little over thirteen years ago." I gasped, and my heart stuck in my throat to think Frankie had been gone so long.

"He is still part of you, Ernest, never forget that. And now he is part of me because you shared his memory with me. You have kept him alive in your memory."

"Oh Frankie, how I miss you so!" I trumpeted loudly.

"Mr. William started this place about twelve years ago. He finds badly mistreated elephants and gives them a home. He probably never wanted what happened to Frankie to happen to any more of us."

"Frankie died way too young. I believe he wanted to."

"Me too, Ernest. Me too."

14

BACHELOR'S FOREST

*You become responsible, for-
ever, for what you have tamed.*
—ANTOINE DE SAINT-EXUPÉRY

MY MOTHER INFORMED me Mr. William founded Bachelor's
Forest to house mistreated captive bull elephants.
The problem with bulls in captivity is our immense
size. We are huge, and most facilities cannot accom-
modate us. Many of us live chained and immobilized
for most of our lives. The humans are afraid of us on
a good day and more than terrified when the surge
of testosterone rears its ugly head. I assumed I was
the fourth to arrive, but later found out, I was actually
the sixth. Two males had died before I arrived. Much
to Mr. William's dismay and broken heart, after years
of horrific conditions, the bulls were too damaged to
thrive once they arrived at Bachelor's Forest. "They

died from *Bad Lung Disease*," my mother, Clementine explained.

"Bad Lung Disease?"

"A deadly disease we contracted from humans. I overhead Mr. William refer to it as TB."

Now the humans are giving us their diseases? Was there any relief from the deadly consequences of being in the world of humans? I could just hear Frankie say, "Good grief, the torture never ends!"

My mother continued, "Grayson and Robert arrived together. Though they did not know each other prior to coming to the forest, they became fast friends. In their mid-twenties, both had lived with all four legs chained for years. Unable to move, unable to turn around, they couldn't lie down, and stood in their own excrement for years! How miserable they must have been!"

I heard of this fate falling on bulls too massive to travel on the road and too dangerous for display at a zoo.

"The sweetest boys," she continued. "Grayson's legs were damaged from the chains being so tight, cutting off his circulation. He literally could not feel his feet. He hobbled around the best he could. Robert, so happy to be unchained, wandered around the forest nonstop for weeks on end, his legs and feet in much better condition than Grayson's. No one knew how sick they were, so great was their joy."

I shuddered to think that could be my fate if not for Mr. William finding me.

"Grayson spent most of his time in the pond. He floated to keep the weight off his feet, eyes usually open, taking in all the sights. Other times he closed his eyes and napped. He always smiled, whether awake or asleep. Another joy he relished was to be able to lie down. He lay on an incline, though, because it was difficult for him to stand back up with his damaged feet. He was with us for about eight months. One day he could not get up, he was so weak. It was his lungs. Mr. William stayed by his side to make sure he had enough water and fed him anything and everything he wanted. An extremely concerned Robert hovered nearby. I could see all this because the pond is near the fence on the north side. The incline even closer to the fence allowed Grayson and me to visit most days. He didn't talk much about his earlier life. He mostly asked questions about the trees, the grass, the birds, and the other elephants. He was delighted to finally see the moon and the stars and sleep under the night sky whenever he wanted to. He proudly walked unchained, and ate whatever he wanted whenever he wanted. Insatiable, wanting to learn all he could, he must have known his time was limited.

"Mr. William made him as comfortable as possible. His breathing had become labored and he had lost his appetite toward the end. When he took his last breath, Grayson had a smile on his sweet face. At least he died knowing kindness. Several months later Robert left us. Having been with us a little over a year, he wandered into the woods one day and never returned. He must have known it was time, and wished to die alone, old soul that he was. Mr. William did say Robert looked very peaceful when he found him. I am thankful he knew peace. Better one day in the forest than a lifetime in captivity." My mother let out a heavy sigh and continued, "I overheard Mr. William talking to one of the humans about finding Robert and cursing TB. Two more souls needlessly lost to the web of captivity." She rumbled softly, "Why can't they just leave us alone?"

My mother's sadness was palpable. When she finished with Robert and Grayson's story, we stood side by side, silent for a very long time, lost in our own thoughts.

***

I STAYED IN my enclosure for a few weeks while I became acquainted with the others. My mother and I spent a lot of time together every day. The rest of the time she spent with her two friends, Edna, whom I affectionately nicknamed Enormous Edna, and Anna, already nicknamed Anna Banana for her expertise at stealing bananas from everyone. Anna and Edna had been friends for a very long time and bonded long before my mother showed up. They finished each other's sentences! I could tell they adored my mother. Who would not? Their faces would light up whenever they saw my mother.

The two elderly ladies were not mother and daughter, but sisters. Calpurnia and Portia had retired from the road after forty years. Forty years! They arrived at Bachelor's Forest a year or so after my mother, and they still looked road weary. Friendly enough, they welcomed me warmly yet most of the time kept to themselves. Calpurnia, the older and the prettier of the two, had a beautiful smile and bright expressive eyes. Portia, though cute and full of mischief, carried an air of sadness with her. Having never been apart their entire lives, they were inseparable. One of their greatest joys was to never have to walk trunk-to-tail in center ring again! As I settled in, they came to visit me now and then but most of the time they made a big fuss over Hank. How they adored him, and he loved them right back.

15

EDWARD

*Kindness is a language the deaf can
hear and the blind can see.*
MARK TWAIN

EDWARD, THE FIRST resident of Bachelor's Forest, wise, sage, dignified, and majestic, he quietly roamed the grounds. He was magnificent, the most imposing elephant I have ever seen, his massive frame towering over all of us. Older than his years, Edward had a weariness about him. Grossly mistreated by humans, his damaged body was battered and bruised from years of abuse. His delicate and wrinkled skin hung loosely from his frame. Not just his body had been damaged. Edward had been wounded deep inside where his internal scars were the most profound. He looked worn out, yet when he spoke, his mighty voice thundered. We were in awe of him. I guessed him to be close to Frankie's age. When I first met Edward, Frankie would have been almost fifty if he had survived.

What stood out the most about Edward, other than his size, were his eyes. Behind them lived a wise old elephant with a gentle soul. When I looked into those eyes, I felt haunted by the untold atrocities that lived in his soul. Just because we are large does not mean we do not appreciate kindness. The majority of humans treat us as evil beasts due to our size, and it was obvious Edward had had more than his share of unkind treatment.

My mother adored Edward. Most days they visited by the fence. His giant tusks continued to grow back after the ends had been sawed off. A true gentleman, he used them to dig up tasty roots near the fence to share with my mother. He never spoke of his life before Bachelor's Forest; he did not have to. It eked out of every fiber of his being. How could he ever articulate the unspeakable? My mother told me Edward was very shy around other elephants, having lived the majority of his life isolated and alone. Yet when she shared her story with Edward, he listened attentively to her tales of suffering. His genuine compassion caused him to weep. And how elated he felt when my mother and I reunited! I approached him tentatively the first time we met, so intimidated by his massive size and majestic presence. He happily showed me around the forest, and officially introduced me to Hank and Bart. A gentle giant, I loved him immediately.

***

EDWARD CERTAINLY KNEW his way around Bachelor's Forest. I remember my first summer, a real scorcher. Edward's sensitive skin did not like too much sun and for months he spent most of the daylight hours in the dense woodlands. Usually he joined the rest of us at the fence around dusk when the sun did not beat down as hot. A couple of times he stayed in the woods all night. The first time I was afraid for him—what if something terrible happened?—My mother eased my concerns. "In the wild, that is perfectly normal behavior, Ernest. Males spend a lot of time on their own, depending on their age. The younger males will seek out an older male to mentor them. The older males do visit their birth families periodically, but seek females outside the family to mate with. Otherwise they spend the majority of their time alone."

Edward invited me to join him one day. We plodded along at a leisurely pace and fed on vegetation on either side of a well-worn path. We tore down branches with our trunks, and then stuffed them in our mouths. Our large feet crunched among the many fallen leaves. I watched Edward rub his back and sides on a tree trunk, so I did the same. I rubbed my body all over the biggest tree I could find. The old established tree did not budge against my five-and-a-half-ton frame. Oh, how wonderful it felt to scratch!

We waded into a shallow pond, and as we stood knee deep in muddy water, I saw frogs everywhere! Though they serenaded me to sleep many a night, I had never seen one before. What odd-looking creatures indeed. Edward scooped up a large chunk of foul-smelling mud with his trunk and hurled it at me. Of course, I returned in kind and a water fight ensued as we squirted each other, using our trunks as giant weapons. I felt that familiar pang for Frankie, who would have been in his element here in Bachelor's Forest. I imagined he and Edward wrestling with their trunks entwined, heads pushed together, as they heaved and grunted from the tension. I was no match for Edward's physique. I guessed him to be close to seven tons, give or take a few hundred pounds; close to the size of Frankie, but much more solid and muscular. I did not realize it when I knew him in the cement prison, but Frankie lacked muscle mass from want of exercise. No wonder he stayed irritable. Imagine six tons of atrophied muscle!

Edward and I eventually splashed out of the water and continued down another well-worn path as the slippery patches of dirt formed shallow pools from our dripping footprints. Leaves and mud stuck in all the nooks and crannies of our loose, wrinkly skin. Edward showed me his favorite napping spot. The ground had an indentation from where he had rested many times before. I felt safe in his company, and the soft ground felt good; I fell into a deep sleep while listening to the sounds of birds, crickets, and frogs.

What a sight we must have been as we emerged from the forest the following afternoon, two dripping, mud soaked giants adorned in green slime and matted wet leaves!

16

HANK

They cherish each other's hopes. They
are kind to each other's dreams.
—HENRY DAVID THOREAU

MY MOTHER WAS right. Hank turned out to be a really nice guy. Without an aggressive bone in his body, we became fast friends. He was twelve years old when we met, a little over half my age and captive born like me. He still missed his mother terribly. Taken from her at age five, he so needed my mother, and loved her with every ounce of his being. How lucky they were to find each other! He told me he did not know what he would have done without her. I shared my feelings about Eve and we bonded instantly, kindred spirits for life. Stocky and big for his age, Hank had a tenderness to him he tried to hide, but it was impossible; one had only to look into his kind eyes to know how sweet-natured he was. We shared our stories by the fence, and when I became integrated into his side of the forest we played and played and played. I fondly named him Hank the Tank. We wrestled, mud-wallowed, stripped bark, napped, grazed, explored, swam, visited with the ladies, and started all over again every day.

We traveled across the open landscape, exploring along the way. At the edge of the forest we stopped and grazed on the lush green grass. Bachelor's Forest was so vast initially I felt I would be swallowed up into nothingness. The largest mammal that walks the earth, I felt like a tiny speck in the universe; so overwhelmed was I by the wide open spaces.

Everything lush and green, water holes that never ran dry, dense woodlands leading to hidden ponds: it all felt like a dream. Every blade of grass, every leaf, every tree, every stream, and even the breeze seemed to welcome me home.

At midday, when the sun was the hottest, most of us mingled under the shade of the two large oak trees, one on each side of the fence. Sometimes we would visit, and other times we would nap or just graze and quietly enjoy the company of one other. I came to love Hank's soft spoken, kind, gentle disposition.

The hills were not very high—mostly gentle slopes—except for one, a small mountain. My mother, Hank, and I trekked to the top early my first spring at the forest. The fence went all the way to the top and back down again. We could see for miles and miles in all directions as the hot sun beat down from a cloudless sky, warming our bodies in the cool spring air. We had a bird's-eye view of the brilliant spring flowers and wide green plains that stretched beyond our sight; new leaves and buds sprouted on the lush forest trees, and long green grasses gently bent in the soft breeze. I saw several ponds, some big and some small. A small stream calmly flowed through the forest; there was no beginning or end to it.

All of this reminded me of the first time I had seen Maggie in paradise. I was a different elephant then; it seemed like such a big place. At only eight years old, the five acres had seemed endless compared to the cement prison I shared with Frankie. I so wished he stood beside me at that moment. Hank and I feasted on a variety of vegetation and bark, and I even dug up some roots with my tusks to share with my mother. As night fell, my mother returned to the others; we watched her get smaller and smaller as she neared the bottom of the hill. Hank and I spent the night under more stars than I had ever seen, twinkling brightly under the still cloudless night sky. The only thing missing was Frankie and Maggie.

17

BART

If animals could talk, mankind would weep.
—Anthony Douglas Williams

Bart was twenty-five years old when I came to Bachelor's Forest. He had been seventeen when he arrived, his pain and grief too severe for words. Broken, disheartened, angry, and hopeless, near starvation, the epitome of sadness, he stayed isolated for years. He could not lie down to sleep because he could not get comfortable—he was so boney. What one noticed immediately about Bart besides his tusklessness was his voice. He sounded nasally all the time, like something was stuck up his trunk. After a while I got used to it; he would not be Bart without that voice. Bart never grew tusks; my mother told me it happened now and then, an accident of nature. When he first arrived to recover from his trauma, he hated everybody and everything. My mother, Hank, Edna, and Anna tried to befriend him, and all he did was glare at them, his eyes the color of deep, dark mud. He constantly challenged Edward, who just ignored him. Anna even tried to share her bananas with him. He hurled them at her with high-pitched trumpets of rage, his ears flared. Soon everyone stayed away from him because he was so wretched.

My mother explained, "Mr. William intuitively knew Bart needed love and respect. He could see beyond the sadness, terror, anger, and defeat. He could see the true soul who lived within. What a waste of an elephant to be chained all day long, unable to move, just standing, doing nothing, a powerful wild animal beaten into submission. The eyes of his heart were shut tight from so much pain. Kind Mr. William worked with Bart, patiently allowing him to show himself when he felt ready. Bart wanted to be recognized as he was, not how humans wanted him to be for their selfish ends. Mr. William could see Bart, and Bart knew it. Soon he began to root, browse, shred, and feast with such vigor we knew he was choosing life and living. He foraged every day and night for months. He began to fill out. His favorite pastimes in the heat of summer were to wallow in mud and take naps all day. He took the greatest pleasure just rolling around in the mud. He still preferred to be alone, though; Edward kept his distance, yet always with an eye on how Bart was doing. Edward's empathy and compassion for Bart started the healing process for both of them.

"Eventually Bart warmed up to Edward. None of us know for sure the atrocities either of them suffered. We can only imagine. They share the unspeakable, and refuse to talk about it except to each other. I watched them show each other every scar on their bodies. The shared understanding of their mutual suffering helped them begin to heal the scars of their psyches. Kindred spirits and almost inseparable for a year, gentle Edward showed Bart how to stop struggling with the whys, to be thankful for and enjoy the life he lives today. There is no way for us to understand the ways of humans. One thing is for certain: Bart's steadfast love for Edward. Bart still has a long way to go. All he ever wanted was for someone to be nice to him. He has started to reach out in his own Bart way, and we will respond in our own way, in kind."

***

THE FIRST TIME I ever actually swam, I swam with Hank. The mud-wallows in paradise with Maggie were not deep; even though all but my head was underwater, my feet always touched ground. In my new home some of the ponds were so deep my feet never touched the bottom. Hank, an adept swimmer, used his trunk as a periscope; disappearing under the muddy water, the only trace of him was the tip of his trunk. I followed his lead. At first I did not close my eyes, and the mud stung. Hank taught me to rinse them off with my trunk, filled with the less muddied water from the top of the pond. We then scooped up large quantities of thick mud and caked it all over ourselves and had a water fight using our trunks as large squirt guns!

In our mayhem we did not notice Bart, who stood nearby and watched us. Bart castrated and without any tusks, at times remained sullen, irritable, and cranky. I had tried to befriend him, but his anger and impatience with me made it difficult to be around him. My mother said he had an inferiority complex.

Bart dust-bathed and seemed to be waiting for an invitation from us. Hank stopped his assault on me and trumpeted for Bart to join us. I too trumpeted an invitation, and surprisingly he accepted. Bart was slightly older than me, taller, and about half a ton heavier. He ran into the pond with a gigantic splash, water and mud flying everywhere! What a ruckus we made. Hank and Bart wrestled, bellowing, splashing, dunking, and rubbing all over each other. Though Hank could have easily won the match, I am sure he let Bart win. It did wonders for Bart's self-confidence; it was the first time Hank and I had ever seen him smile. Later, as we left to meet the others by the fence, Bart had a spring to his step. Hank told me later he had indeed let Bart win, because "it was the manly elephant thing to do." I did not understand what he meant at the time.

18

EDNA

*But there is something in human
depravity which, I think, far exceeds
anything to be seen in the behavior of animals.*
—CHRISTOPHER NICHOLSON

A FEW MONTHS after I settled into my new life, one warm brightly moonlit night, my mother and I snacked on the delicious grass near the fence. She shared Edna's story. Edna, like most of us, was a rescued elephant. For almost fifteen years she existed as the only elephant in a traveling roadside zoo suffering horrifying abuse, until she was eventually abandoned. Fifteen years! I thought of Frankie and his five years at a barren roadside zoo; that was bad enough.

When I met Edna she was thirty-three years old. A kind, sweet soul and a very beautiful elephant, the scar on her face did not take away from her beauty.

Such an absolute joy to be around, it was hard to fathom where she had come from.

"It took Edna a long time to recover from the terror and abuse she suffered," my mother snorted. "She was rescued twelve years ago, and is profoundly thankful to be here. Someone abandoned her in a trailer at the trash dump." She flapped her ears resentfully.

"Someone threw away a live elephant?" I bellowed incredulously. Humans never ceased to amaze me.

"A bag of bones covered with gaping wounds, her skin hung loosely on her frame, her trunk partially paralyzed from unspeakable cruel treatment. Beyond terrified, she struck out at anybody or anything that came close to her."

I was afraid to ask how she received the huge gash on her beautiful face.

"Labeled as 'dangerous', her life before being abandoned and found in a discarded trailer was one of horrific cruelty."

"Good grief. As if being abandoned and thrown away wasn't cruel enough!" I could hear Frankie grumble in annoyance. I shuddered to think of the unspeakable treatment Edna received. Where does the desire to maliciously harm another come from? We elephants are kind, gentle souls, and there is nothing in elephant society that remotely resembles the brutal side of human nature.

My mother continued, "Some kind soul noticed her trunk sticking out of the trailer and called the authorities. She was pathetic. Dead animals all around her, it took months for the stench of death to leave her trunk and years for it to leave her mind. An absolutely frightening experience!"

I knew Edna had been rescued and lived at the forest for a good while, but I had no idea her past was *that* harrowing. She seemed so easygoing in her pleasant, caring, and concerned manner.

"Your Mr. William," my mother continued, "patiently worked with her. Edna was extremely skittish and nervous, so scared she trembled. Look at her now: so affectionate, so sweet-natured. But only to Mr. William and her own kind. It took years for her to learn to trust again. She won't tolerate any other humans, and she refuses to talk about it anymore. So please don't mention I told you her story."

I felt so sorry for Edna, who really did have a sweet disposition. Highly intelligent and stunningly beautiful, I never would have guessed in a million years she had had it so bad. She adjusted well, though—another survivor of the ignorance of humans. "Thank you, Mr. William," I sighed loudly. "Poor Edna."

"Don't feel sorry for her, Ernest. She doesn't need pity. Share her joy that she is here with us, far away from the savagery she once knew. Let's celebrate that she is healing and able to experience love and kindness in her life. There is something to be said for the intense, quiet joy of being alive."

Trees swayed in unison as a gentle wind blew through their branches. My mother raised her head to enjoy the soft breeze on her face.

"I so wish Frankie was here to talk to," I whispered to my mother as we said good night.

Her tired, sad eyes looked at me with one of those all-knowing Eve looks and she tenderly hugged me with her trunk. She turned to head back to her barn, and as I watched her slowly disappear over the top of the hill, I felt saddened and cheated out of all the years we missed being together as a family. A speckled butterfly danced by and landed on the tip of my trunk. I could not remember ever seeing a butterfly at night before.

19

Anna

The First Duty of Love is to Listen.
-Paul Tillich

Anna had an edge to her. She reminded me of Mary, the most standoffish of all the ladies. Not that she was unlikable—in fact, she was very well thought of by the others—but she did have a bit of a hard shell around her, making it difficult to get close to her at times. She really liked my mother and Edna. Sometimes she visited with Calpurnia and Portia, but most times she hung out with Edna and my mother. She had no interest in any of the males at all. I do not know much about her previous life other than she was grossly underweight when she arrived at Bachelor's Forest. When I met her she was forty years old and had come to the forest five years earlier. True to her name, a master at stealing bananas, and could be chewing on a bunch before the victim ever knew they were gone!

One day as my mother and I enjoyed a quiet morning by the fence, Anna and Edna lumbered over to join us. Anna and I grazed on the tender fresh grass as my mother and Edna visited with each other.

My mother rumbled, "Anna has rounded out nicely, hasn't she?"

"Indeed," chirped Edna good-naturedly, "I will have to keep a better eye on my bananas!"

"You know, Edna, it wouldn't hurt you to lose a few pounds!" Anna growled.

Hurt by the insult, Edna looked away and rumbled something under her breath.

"Anna, you are too hard on her," scolded my mother.

"She really has gotten fat with all those bananas she won't share!"

"Anna, you are not petite! Edna has been more than generous with her bananas. You must make amends."

Anna stripped a large piece of bark off a tree and begrudgingly headed toward Edna. My mother sighed at Anna's abrasiveness. "Some cause happiness wherever they go, others whenever they go!"

It was not long before Anna and Edna exchanged trunk hugs.

***

LATE ONE LAZY afternoon, as Bart, Hank, and I awoke from our afternoon naps, thunder roared in the distance. Hank stood up quickly, his eyes wide with fear, and ran as fast as he could back toward the barn. The thunder terrified him, something to do with when he was on the road. No matter how hard he tried to shrug it off as nothing, he could not help himself from being traumatized by his past. The rest of us stood under one of the giant oaks by the fence, where my mother joined us.

Laughing, I asked my mother, "What is wrong with Hank? I have never seen him move so fast. He is practically running."

My mother answered sweetly, "When he was very young, Hank had a hard time understanding one of the commands from his human handler. In his confusion and fear of reprisal, he froze. He couldn't move. First the human tried to coax him, and then hit him hard with the sharp end of the bull hook. More confused and scared, he peed all over himself. This prompted more beating. Humiliated, Hank began to cry. Another human passing by stopped the beating and tried to console Hank, who by now was sobbing uncontrollably. The human continued to calm Hank, and gently led him to a stall and chained him up for the rest of the day. Worn out, he dozed standing up, unable to lie down due the chains.

"Some kids snuck into the elephant area and threw firecrackers at the elephants getting ready to perform. The deafening noise made Hank fear for his life. He thrashed and kicked and screamed, unable to escape. Elephants scattered everywhere. Some ran into the arena, others the parking lot. Hank could not get away. People ran amok, screaming. Needless to say, there was no performance that day. Hours later, all the elephants were eventually captured and returned to their stalls. Meanwhile, Hank was still traumatized and trapped in his chains. Whenever he hears thunder, the noise triggers a horrible memory and he runs for cover."

Bart told me later he tried to make fun of Hank to toughen him up. He thought he was helping him. Edward put a stop to that. "Under no circumstances," he thundered, "do we make fun of another's suffering. Each of us must cope in our own way. Do we not strive for self-respect and respect for all? Or is it every elephant for himself? Always be kind, we are all struggling. Never look away, even if you don't know how to help. The first duty of love is to listen. We must have compassion for all living beings. By not listening and responding we disconnect ourselves from a large part of our elephantness, and that is not right. Look others in the eye and acknowledge their suffering!"

Poor Hank. I felt bad to think he had endured such horror. And such a sweet little guy. Well, not little anymore, at twelve years old he weighed over four tons and already taller than my mother.

20

LIVING ON ELEPHANT TIME

There can be no vulnerability without risk. There can be no community without vulnerability. There can be no peace, and ultimately no life, without community.
-M. SCOTT PECK

AT FIRST I could not put a name to it. As I found my place in the forest I began to notice an obvious lack of human intervention. I was sometimes aware of Mr. William on the periphery, but he rarely interacted with me, and only if I initiated it. The first few weeks I had seen him several times a day because he would check on me. He remained on the sidelines and adopted a hands-off approach. Because I was captive born, there had never been a time in my life I had not been dependent on a human for food and water. The most freedom I ever experienced was in paradise with

Maggie. We played all day unlike on the road, but still were put to bed at night and chained by a human.

At the forest, several barns were available to us if we wanted shelter, or we could stay out all day and night; the choice was ours. At first I felt uncomfortable, having been told what to do all my life. My life revolved around a human schedule, not an elephant schedule. And it felt amazing not being on display or having to perform. I thought about how much Frankie hated being stared at all day long. I so wished he could be with me.

I remember the first night I slept outside under the stars at the forest with no human bringing me in for the night. It had been dark for several hours as Hank and I grazed near the fence my second week at the forest. Hank stopped eating and looked up at the sky. "There are more stars out tonight than I have ever seen before. What do you know about stars, Ernest?"

"I know just because you cannot see them does not mean they are not there. I know each one represents those of us who have gone before."

"Tonight a lot of dead elephants are represented. Look at all those stars!" Hank trumpeted sadly and flared his ears.

"We have roamed the earth for thousands of years. Frankie told me his family traveled the same migratory paths as his ancestors for thousands and thousands of years. The matriarchs pass important information from generation to generation."

Hank sighed. "I miss my mom. I wonder what happened to her."

I reached through the fence with my trunk to comfort him. I knew all too well how he felt. Not knowing was the worst part. He could not grieve in finality and remained in an emotional limbo. We stayed together in silence for several hours, enjoying each other's company. After a while, Hank decided to go to sleep and lay down by the fence. Tired and weary myself, I decided to do the same. I fell into a deep sleep. For the second time in my life, I slept unchained under the stars.

After a few weeks, I moved to the male side of the forest. Other than feeling a bit overwhelmed, I felt no fear. No fear—an odd feeling indeed; yet at the same time it all seemed oddly familiar, as if buried deep in my mind as some long forgotten memory.

It did not happen all at once. It took a while. As I resolved to take each precious moment and relish all the joy in it, I slowly started to discover my elephant-ness. Some days I would close my eyes and deeply breathe in the clean, fresh air. As my breath expanded my chest cavity, my heart expanded and opened. Sometimes I felt tenderness for all living beings, and other times I felt sadness for all that had happened to me and the others. I remembered Eve telling me, "Approaching life with an open heart returns us to our true selves. We are meant to love, Ernest. When you find compassion in your heart for all living beings, you know you are on your way to healing." As always, she had been right.

One of the things that struck me the most was the singing of the birds. I cannot remember if I woke to their morning song when in paradise with Maggie, but I do not remember ever hearing a bird sing while on the road. There had been no singing at the breeding center or at the zoo with Eve. At least, I do not remember any. I wished Eve and Maggie were with me so I could ask them. Now each morning, right before dawn, I hear a lone peep, and then another peep would answer; the peeps grow louder as the sky becomes brighter, then lots of peeps and chirps slowly working up to a crescendo of happy sounds. This became one of my favorite times of the day.

Hank showed me the "sandbox," an extremely large mound of sand more than three times as tall as Edward. We lay in it and rolled around, then climbed to the top and slid down on our butts. Sometimes we rolled down the sand pile and landed in a heap on top of each other, laughing, and sand everywhere—in our eyes, mouths, trunks, and ears! We would then jump into the nearby pond and loudly bellow our merriment. Sometimes Bart joined us as we threw mud and dunked each other.

Another day, the three of us covered in sand from head to toe, were about to wade into the pond. As we laughed and carried on, we did not see the snorkel that was Edward's trunk. He must have heard us, because he popped up out of the pond like a jack-in-the-box and startled us all so much we lost our footing and fell into the pond. Trunks, legs, feet, ears, and tails everywhere! We slid and sputtered all over the place, unable to get our footing as Edward watched in amusement. I love the way he always laughs with his eyes.

***

THE DAYS DRIFTED by, each one melting into another. With the arrival of another summer, the weather stayed hot and muggy. No breeze and the air so thick you could cut it with a knife. The ponds were like glass, not even a tiny ripple. The deer lay listlessly in the shade of the mighty oaks, their little tails not even twitching. The birds were silent, probably napping in a cool shady spot.

One day, Bart and Edward grazed near the largest pond under a giant elm tree. Hank and I tried to nap in the shade, but the flies persistently bit us.

"Let's go cool off in the pond and get some mud to ward off these flies." Hank rumbled.

We trudged down to the pond and I stopped in my tracks as we were about to wade in. I looked in the pond to see two elephants staring back at us. I did not recognize one of them, but the other looked just like Hank. I looked at Hank, who was making figure eights with his trunk, then glanced back at the elephant in the pond, who was imitating him, then back at Hank, who was laughing at me. The elephant who looked like Hank began to laugh. I trumpeted at the other elephant, and he trumpeted back, yet without a sound. Bart and Edward walked over to see what the commotion was about, and as they stopped at the edge of the pond, two more elephants appeared on the water's surface. They looked exactly like Bart and Edward! And they too laughed. I peered into the face of the elephant I did not recognize; our eyes met and I realized I was seeing myself for the first time. As I smiled in recognition, my reflection smiled back at me.

The four of us stayed in the pond most of the afternoon as the sun beat down on us with unforgiving intensity. What a joy to be able to cool off in a refreshing pond! I remembered the suffocating boxcars at the height of the summer. How had we ever survived such torment?

We splashed around and dunked each other for a while and for most of the afternoon quietly stayed afloat to remain cool. Hank and Bart left the pond before Edward and me, but not before they rolled around in the shallow end to cover themselves in mud from head to toe. They grazed nearby as we continued to float, the feeling of weightlessness relaxing. The sun moved to the other side of the forest, and butterflies visited the flowers, fluttering from one to the next. We enjoyed watching the birds chase each other through the treetops, chirping loudly. The sun was still bright in the late afternoon sky and the birds began to sing again.

Edward and I covered ourselves in mud before we left the pond, now on a mission to satisfy our growing hunger. It is hard to explain the feeling of being able to eat when hungry—or to not eat when not hungry. Ravenous, we grazed for hours until the sun began to set. The birds became silent as the frogs and crickets started their nightly competition. The heat made us all tired, and as the air cooled a bit without the unrelenting sun, Hank and Bart lay down on their sides and were fast asleep as soon as their heads hit the ground. Edward and I laughed as they snored loudly.

We would repeat this routine for many months during the heat wave. I said good night to Edward and walked to the fence to see my mother. I missed her, as I had not seen her since the day before.

By the time I made it to the fence, my mother, Calpurnia, and Portia were already fast asleep under the giant oak. The heat must have been hard on them too, as they were covered in mud from head to toe. Elephants have sensitive skin; without bathing and covering our skin with mud and dirt, our skin can become damaged. Mary had once told me mud aids our skin by regulating our body temperature and makes good sunscreen and moisturizer. Ah, Mary.

My mother snored softly, and as I watched her sleep, a great tenderness washed over me. Though we were practically strangers, I loved her as only a small child can love his mother. She looked so beautiful and peaceful as she slept, and I thought of all the empty years I had been without her. I wondered where Anna and Edna were. The full moon cast enough light for me to see Edward standing at the top of the giant hill, looking rather majestic. He was still a little shy, and I loved being in his company; he had the same calming influence as Eve. I wondered how she was doing. I really missed her, and wished she could see the forest. I know she and Edward would become fast friends, and wondered if their paths ever crossed.

A warm breeze washed over me, and my weariness finally caught up with me. I lay down at the fence and as I fell into a deep slumber, a lone butterfly landed on my trunk.

I slept soundly that night and dreamed of Maggie and me, with Frankie and Eve, living free in the wild. They introduced Maggie and me to their families at a large watering hole. Elephants everywhere, and Frankie the happiest I had ever seen him!

***

GONE WAS THE feeling of constantly being watched. Some days I looked for Mr. William and he was nowhere to be found. How odd, I thought. Every day, I felt more and more like an elephant and less and less like a piece of property. Edward told me the humans consider us objects because they think we cannot talk.

"We talk all the time!" I protested.

"They don't understand our language because it is different from theirs. Humans think we lack consciousness."

"That makes no sense."

"We are a means to the human end. They view us as commodities. They do not realize we are capable of suffering, just like them."

"Mr. William knows who and what we are. He knows we think and feel."

"He is the exception," Edward snorted, flapping his ears. "However, though we have a good life at

Bachelor's Forest, we still remain in captivity. Humans think they are helping us by giving us bigger enclosures. Why are we even in an enclosure in the first place?"

He had a point. Not that I was complaining about my new home.

"We have the right not to be treated as property. Ever wonder why we are separated from the ladies?"

"To be honest, I was so thankful to have access to the ladies through the fence I had not given it much thought. Why?"

"So we don't breed."

"Why not?"

"Elephants are not indigenous to Bachelor's Forest. Mr. William does not want any more elephants born in captivity. Which is a good thing, yet we are still unable to exhibit all our natural behaviors."

I remembered my mother saying, "This is as good as it gets *in captivity*." I looked deep into Edward's eyes. "Have you ever fathered a child?" He looked at me intently for a good long while. Finally, he sighed. "Yes, twice. Both boys. They died before they were two years old. Mr. William is right; captive breeding is a bad thing."

And that was the end of the conversation. I knew better than to ask any more questions. Bart later told me wherever Edward had been before he came to the forest was a terrible place for elephants, especially babies.

***

EDWARD WAS THE biggest loner of the group, with Bart a close second. Though there were times when I preferred to be by myself, Hank and I were the least likely to be alone. We both enjoyed the company of the ladies, and I felt an urgency to see my mother every day. She told me that was not the way of the wild, however, and males see their mothers rarely. Most days she stayed busy socializing with all the other ladies. I only wanted to make up for lost time.

So Hank and I spent a lot of time together. We looked forward to our special times with Edward, and tolerated Bart, though I must say Bart became easier to be around as time passed. Something about him made him quite lovable yet at the same time not so lovable. An especially needy elephant, he tried awfully hard not to be. There was something extremely poignant about Bart. Awkward around other elephants, taken from his mother much too young, he had spent a large amount of time chained in solitary confinement.

Most mornings Hank and I met the others by the fence under the oak trees. We said our good mornings to all, and grazed for hours and hours before our daily mud-baths. Shortly after I arrived at the forest, a tan cat greeted me each morning as he sat on top of one of the fence posts. He reminded me of my lion friend at the zoo from so long ago, though he was much smaller. I wondered what ever happened to my friend with the saddest eyes, whose life had been nothing more than endless pacing in his bleak cement prison.

Here in Bachelor's Forest, Cat, as he came to be known, followed Hank and me wherever we went in the forest. He constantly rubbed up against us, and purred incredibly loud. At first we thought him a tremendous pest, this little creature we could send flying with a small flick of our trunks. But he soon ingratiated himself to us, curling up against one or the other on cool nights. He kept his distance during our mudbaths, and then pranced along happily as we climbed up and down the rolling hills. His favorite annoying trick was to climb a tree and then pounce on us as we walked by. I was just beginning to think he was such a sweet little guy when I had a rude awakening.

Hank and I napped on the side of one of the hills late one morning, when a distressed shriek woke us up. Much to our surprise and dismay, Cat had a struggling bird in his mouth. Feathers flew in all directions from Cat's mouth as the terrified bird fought for her life. Undaunted, Cat held her between his paws and bit her neck. Silence. He then proceeded to make a meal out of her.

Hank and I stared, horrified. We elephants eat a lot all day long, most days 200 pounds or more of food. But we never eat flesh. As herbivores, we only eat fruits, grass, bark, mud, hay, roots, dirt, twigs, and branches. After Cat finished his meal, he looked very pleased with himself. Our little friend, a predator!

Seven years after my arrival at the forest, Cat disappeared. One day he sat on the fence post, waiting for us, and the next day he disappeared. I saw other cats around the forest, but they never came near us.

I always wondered what happened to him. Perhaps a giant bird ate him.

***

EVERY MORNING WE looked forward to the first wonderful hint of sunlight and fresh air as the energy flowed in hushed tones of promises for another day. We took pleasure in the simple knowledge we had been given the gift of another day without cement, steel bars, bull hooks, or chains. And though not completely liberated, we had the freedom to choose how we spent our days. And that, as my mother said, was as good as it could get in captivity. When the sun first peeked over the horizon, we quietly rose as the earth awakened and embraced the joy of just being and looked forward to another peaceful, fulfilling day. Having seen more than enough pain and suffering to last many lifetimes, deep sleep temporarily washed away the indignities we had previously endured. And though some of us experienced a lingering weariness and stiffness of joints, once we started moving, our vitality returned as the sound of the serenading birds grew richer and richer by the minute. Every day was a gift, and we knew it. Most days some of us stayed on the move up to eighteen hours. Elephants are designed to graze and graze we did—in between naps, of course. We loved the sunshine, the blue skies, our friends, the sense of family, and the smiles. Elephants have a basic need to live as part of a family group in a natural habitat. We love to socialize. Finally allowed to just *be*, we lived our lives unburdened by exploitation. Serenity, at last!

It had been a little over a year since I had joined the fold at Bachelor's Forest and settled into a routine. A routine that helped me learn to live as an elephant on elephant time. Not human time, not even Mr. William time. As I experienced my elephantness more and more, the atrocities of captivity become even more bewildering. And I could not help but ask, why?

***

EDWARD FELT THE vibration of the big truck first. Then Bart. Hank and I napping on the hillside, awakened next. As Hank and I stood up to join Edward and Bart, we actually heard the rumbling, which meant it was close. As expected, we all headed toward the barn to greet the newcomer. There had been no additions since my arrival, less than two years earlier, and excitement and nervousness filled the air. I noticed the ladies almost running to the barn as we rounded the bend. Bart, Hank, Edward, and I stood at the fence, wondering who would come out of the door. It was not long before we saw the large truck enter the forest and Edward began to pace. Apparently he always paced when someone new arrived. So many finally made it to the forest in such terrible shape; it could be heart-wrenching.

I noticed my mother and Calpurnia pacing with anticipation as the door to the truck finally opened.

Out jumped Mr. William, immediately followed by a skeleton-skinny female. I heard the ladies collective gasp. Without delay, another female emerged from the truck; she did not appear to be in such bad shape. They were led to the holding area where I had stayed not so long ago. There were mounds of hay and hundreds of bananas spread about, which both ladies inhaled in minutes, the food immediately replenished by Mr. William. My mother, Calpurnia, Portia, Anna, and Edna stood exactly in the same spot as they had on the day I arrived.

Hank and I started to walk over to greet the newcomers when another, very young, female emerged from the truck. Obviously terrified, she could not have been more than ten years old. As she sucked her trunk, I immediately identified with the fear in her eyes, her ears spread wide. I wanted to reach out and hug her. Mr. William gently coaxed her toward the others. Her terror palpable, I could almost hear her heart pounding. Her knees locked and she could not move. Mr. William offered her some bananas; she refused. It took well over an hour for her to enter the holding area. Once in, she ran screaming toward the others, who welcomed and embraced her with their trunks.

21

Elephants For Rent

The only good cage is an empty cage.
—Lawrence Anthony

Suzanna, Izzie, and Alberta had belonged to an elephant rental company, where they lived in deplorable conditions.

"Elephant *Rental Company*?" snorted Edward as he flapped his ears.

I could hear Frankie: "Good grief, now the humans have stooped to *renting* elephants!"

"Elephant Rental Company?" Edward repeated several times, trying to grasp the concept.

Suzanna, headstrong, proud, and the oldest, at twenty-five, had become angry at her cruel mistreatment. The angrier she became, the worse her treatment. Food and water withheld, and all four of her legs had been chained tightly together, causing her to almost go mad. She had open wounds all over her emaciated body when she first arrived at Bachelor's Forest. Her tormentor had gone too far one day when he beat Alberta, the youngest, who at nine years old accidently defecated before breakfast rather than afterward. Izzie, at twenty, had managed to stay fed by always obeying every command, no matter how painful. However, this time the human underestimated his supremacy, and Izzie grabbed him with her trunk and slammed his body into the cement wall of their prison. Suzanna then scooped him up with her trunk and hurled him into the air. After he landed with a very loud thud, they took turns stomping him into a bloody pulp.

"Overkill? I think not," Edward commented thoughtfully, flapping his ears as he heard the story one afternoon soon after they arrived.

"He *so* deserved it," my mother nodded adamantly.

Calpurnia and Portia silently nodded in unison. Edna shook her head. "Those poor girls, those poor girls." Anna stared blankly without comment; her eyes welled up with tears.

Hank cried; Bart and I listened to their story in horror.

***

FOR MONTHS, SUZANNA did not seem social at all as she voraciously ate everything in sight. The only time she did not eat was when she slept. At first, she could not lie down to sleep because she was so thin; she was unable to get comfortable because her bones stuck out so much, and her feet and legs were damaged from the tight chains she had lived in.

Izzie, a shy little elephant, weighed no more than three tons and had the sweetest disposition. She took to Calpurnia and Portia right away, who adored her, and could not keep their trunks off her. Alberta did not have a shy bone in her cute little body. Outgoing, and not beautiful, yet extremely cute, she immediately won all our hearts. The most social of us all, she ended up as a rental elephant when her mother died in childbirth at a local zoo. The rental company owned an elephant who had just given birth to a stillborn little girl the week before. Still lactating, she immediately and enthusiastically accepted Alberta. After she was weaned, Alberta never saw her surrogate mother again; one day she was there, and the next she was gone. Within days Izzie arrived, and months later Suzanna joined the group of elephants.

"Rented out to do what?" Edward asked curiously. His ears flapping.

"We starred in TV shows and commercials. We were used for elephant rides at carnivals and fairs and birthday parties. Sometimes we attended weddings."

"Astonishing!" Edward trumpeted, still trying to grasp the concept of renting an elephant.

"When we weren't rented out we stayed chained in a very dark and dreary place, barely seeing the light of day," Alberta rumbled, shaking her head sadly, "The darkness, the monotony, the silence made us desperate; the isolation intolerable. Our feet and legs ached from standing on the hard surface. The worst part was when the humans blowtorched the hairs off our bodies before they rented us out. We cried out in terror."

"Why on earth?" Edward asked, horrified.

"So our skin would be nice and smooth."

Edward was rendered speechless after her comment. I could hear Frankie: "Good grief, now we can't even have hair on our bodies because the humans don't like it?"

Alberta faced the open sky. "The warm sun feels so good," she trumpeted, flapping her ears contentedly.

My mother taught Alberta how to mud-wallow and dust-bathe. Alberta loved the feel of mud on her dry sensitive skin. She did not need to be taught how to graze; it came naturally. Alberta giggled delightedly when Edward and I shared the roots we dug up for my mother and her. She savored every bite.

Alberta reminded me of Maggie in the way she loved everybody and everything. She woke up every morning happy and excited about the gift of another day of freedom and choice. She skipped about like a young child, and brought tremendous joy to all of us.

Suzanna began to fill out after several months, and quickly lost the sunken gauntness in her face. "And a mighty fine face, at that," Edward would say. Suzanna made me think of Mary. I so wished Mary had had the opportunity to fill out and be beautiful once again. Suzanna and Izzie remained a pretty solid twosome, though they reached out to the rest of us in friendship. Alberta flitted about like a butterfly from group to group on a daily basis.

For almost six months after they arrived, Suzanna and Izzie were intimidated by the vast open spaces. But eventually they felt confident enough to undertake a journey, so one morning after breakfast they ventured deep into the woodlands with Anna and Edna. Alberta stayed back and hung out with my mother, Calpurnia, and Portia. The four of them spent most of the day in the mud-wallows with ears flapping because the bugs were particularly annoying.

The foursome emerged from the forest as the sun began to set. Side by side, their silhouette loomed large across the horizon among the purple, orange, and pink hues of the setting sun and is a picture I will remember forever. For a moment I felt as if I had witnessed a scene from the wild as the foursome walked shoulder to shoulder across the forested horizon. Ears flapping, trunks gently swinging from side to side, their magnificent bodies gracefully ambled toward the rest of us as we watched with awed respect. I witnessed the strength, beauty, and elegance of their majestic elephantness. As they came closer, I could see their weariness. Suzanna and Izzie had never walked as far, nor as long, their entire lives added together. Exhausted with their heads held high, their splendor glowed in the evening light and they experienced their individual and collective magnificence for the first time in their lives.

The four comrades slept hard that night. My mother, Alberta, and I watched them sleep soundly while we stayed up late and enjoyed the warm glow from the full moon. Suzanna and Izzie snored the loudest, with Anna and Edna a close second. We hoped they enjoyed wonderful elephant dreams. Soon Alberta fell asleep standing up. My mother lay down near the others; I nudged Alberta to do the same. She groggily snuggled up to my mother and soon they were both snoring with the others. It had been a fantastic day for all. I soon lay down under the giant oak and dreamed the most wonderful elephant dreams.

***

LIFE REMAINED PRETTY routine for the rest of the summer. The "fearless foursome," as we began to call the forest dwellers, ventured into the bowels of the forest almost daily. Every now and then, they stayed and swam in the ponds with the rest of us. Izzie loved the mud, and stayed coated from head to toe most of the time when the weather stayed hot. And flies were everywhere! I do not remember seeing so many flies in one place. I remember how much Frankie hated the flies biting him: "Good grief, I am being eaten alive by flies! If only we had mud in this desolate cement prison. I am miserable!" And he was. I am not sure if he was madder at the flies or the lack of mud. Oh Frankie, I wish you were here where we have more than enough mud!

***

AS THE SUN began to set later in the day toward the end of my third summer in Bachelor's Forest, I always looked to the horizon for the "fearless foursome."

When they did not immediately appear one evening, I wondered if they planned to stay out all night. No big deal; Hank and I did so every now and then. I had stayed out all night a few times with Edward, but never with Bart, though I am not sure why. Alberta usually completed her nightly rounds at the fence with me and my mother. This night the ground was extra soft after a late afternoon heavy shower. Edward and I dug up roots as fast as we—and my mother and Alberta—could eat them. The moon was new, so after the sun went down, it became pitch black. Only a handful of stars could be seen. I ate so many roots I thought I would burst. I lay down for a nap. When I awoke in the still darkness, Edward had departed and my mother and Alberta slept soundly. Calpurnia and Portia must have gone back to the barn. Still no sign of the "fearless foursome". I detected two lumps on the hillside to be Bart and Hank sleeping. I grazed a while before going back to sleep.

I awoke with a start to the sound of frantic trumpeting. Anna and Edna ran from the forest, trumpeting their heads off. I could not understand what they were saying. Alberta started to cry. Edward deciphered their message: "Suzanna, after a meal of delicious bark, collapsed and did not have the strength to get back up. Izzie unsuccessfully tried to help her get to her feet. Anna and Edna both tried in vain. Her battered body gave out, unable to recover from the years of neglect and mistreatment. Her three friends by her side, she died peacefully as she lay comfortably in the bed of the forest."

"Where is Izzie now?" asked Alberta.

"She won't leave Suzanna; they tried to get her to come back with them, but she couldn't tear herself away," Edward answered with a deep rumble.

"You two get some rest," he commanded Anna and Edna. "Clementine and I will go to her."

Alberta paced and paced for hours in their absence. I tried to console her, as did Calpurnia and Portia, who eventually persuaded her to go for a swim. Anna and Edna, exhausted, fell asleep soundly after they stuffed themselves at breakfast.

I joined Bart and Hank at the pond and floated with them for hours without speaking. Lost in my thoughts, they left me alone. I felt sad for Alberta and Izzie. Poor Suzanna, another casualty at the hands of humans. When would it ever end?

I left Bart and Hank and returned to the fence at dusk. Alberta, who had returned before me, continued to pace back and forth.

"Edward and my mother will bring her back," I rumbled soothingly.

She stopped and looked at me, then continued to pace.

"Death is part of life." I tried the philosophical approach.

This time she neither stopped nor looked at me.

I joined her in her pacing, side by side, back and forth along the fence. The ladies quietly grazed by the stream, Bart and Hank again two lumps asleep on the hillside.

Not until the following morning did we see the three of them walk slowly out of the forest across the horizon. Edward towered over both my mother and Izzie as he led them, my mother and Izzie shoulder to shoulder behind Edward on their side of the fence.

Izzie, exhausted from several days without sleep, fell into a deep slumber on the hillside. My mother told me they buried Suzanna with leaves, sticks, and twigs, and paid their final respects. Izzie, devastated, had stood guard over her good friend for two days before they could coax her away.

Two weeks later, Izzie went to sleep one night by the fence and never woke up. The cause of death was unknown. Frankie was right, the torture never ends.

***

Sweet Alberta continued to have a hard time accepting her friends were gone. After six months she was still glued to my mother, following her everywhere she went. She cried herself to sleep for months. I missed Frankie and Eve more than usual during these times; they would have been able to put it all in perspective for us. For months after the deaths of Suzanna and Izzie, Edward preferred to be alone. Actually, I did too, other than a daily check-in with my mother and Alberta.

Bart and Hank wandered the forest regularly, walking at least thirty miles each day. I grazed all day long, between dust baths, and enjoyed my solitude.

The warmth of the sun felt good, the spring air still cool. The ladies stayed close to Alberta and my mother, concerned about Alberta's well-being. During one of the morning visits with my mother, she told me, "Alberta is worried about the other three elephants left at the rental company. She is afraid for them. They are young males and handled much more roughly than the females."

"Mr. William would not help three and leave the rest," I said. "Besides, he created Bachelor's Forest for captive males. Even so, Mr. William would never say no to females in need."

During this conversation, we felt the vibration of not one but two big trucks. My mother and I exchanged glances. The other ladies, already headed toward the barn, obviously felt them too. Bart and Hank were already on their way, while Edward slowly plodded down the hill as my mother, Alberta, and I made our way to welcome the newcomers. All of us excited and nervous as usual.

We arrived at the barn before the trucks and waited almost an hour before they arrived. Edward paced, and so did Bart. Hank and I grazed as we waited. I looked across at the ladies and saw Alberta pacing while the others grazed patiently. Finally the two large trucks pulled in.

Edward flapped his ears and softly rumbled, "This is the first time two trucks arrived together. I wonder what's up."

The door of the first truck opened, and Mr. William jumped out. Loud, shrill trumpets boomed from inside. Mr. William ran over to open the door of the second truck while the trumpeting continued in the first. Alberta became agitated and trumpeted back. Mr. William opened the gate to the holding area, already filled with the usual hay and bananas. He then led two very young boys off the second truck. I guessed them both to be about three or four. I could tell they were scared out of their minds because they trembled in fear. Absolutely adorable, both sucked their trunks as Mr. William led them to the food. Meanwhile, the others' trumpets continued, even more distressed. Alberta became hysterical and trumpeted her head off. This went on for a good half hour until two young teenage male elephants emerged from the truck. Finally! By this time Alberta could not contain herself and tried to climb the fence. My mother gently scolded and calmed her, then led her to the holding area fence. The two older boys ran over to Alberta for a joyous reunion of squeals, trumpets, shrieks, and bellows as they peed all over themselves and each other.

Mr. William led the little ones over to the female side of the holding area. It was then I came to find out they were both almost six years old and grossly underweight. Yogi and BooBoo came from a substandard zoo. Some humans complained to the zoo about all the animals' ill-treatment. Mr. William got wind of it and brought them to the forest. In the meantime he finagled a deal to get the remaining elephants from the rental company. Unfortunately, one of them did not make it.

Yogi and BooBoo voraciously ate all their bananas before greeting the ladies. I watched them from my side of the fence.

Edward shook his head sadly. "I hope they make it. I have seen this happen too many times. We are locked behind steel bars in a barren prison at the mercy of humans for food. Completely dependent, we cannot even feed ourselves!" He snorted his indignation, flapped his ears, and walked away. Hank, Bart, and I hung around a little while longer, and then also left. I would hear about them in the morning from my mother.

***

ALBERTA DID NOT come back that night, nor did we see her for several days and nights afterward. She stayed near the holding area with her good friends. She had not seen them in over two years and had missed them very much.

My mother and Edna checked on the two little guys several times a day. Bart and Hank continued to roam the forest daily. Edward still preferred his solitude. About a week later, Alberta visited my mother and me at breakfast time. She looked a little bleary-eyed and terribly sad. She hugged my mother tightly with her trunk and cried for almost an hour. I felt completely helpless and stood there quietly, not knowing what to do. My mother tenderly rubbed Alberta's back while she sobbed. When she could finally speak,

Alberta filled us in on what happened after she left the elephant rental company.

"Little Andy, the youngest of us all, did not obey the human during a training session so he was shocked with an electric prod. Whenever the human came anywhere near Little Andy, he defecated—he was so terrified of the prod. It carried 220 volts of electricity! The next time Little Andy responded incorrectly to a command, one of the humans hosed him off with water then shocked him again with 220 volts. I can't imagine his screams of pain and terror. The second time they hosed him off, he screamed when he saw the prod, even before the electricity went through his body. Once shocked, he died instantly. Owen and Oscar still can't get the smell of his burned body out of their memory. His tortured screams will haunt them forever."

My mother's eyes held mine as her trunk hugged Alberta. We could not speak to this atrocity. We still cannot and question the senselessness of another death.

Owen and Oscar, Alberta's two remaining friends, became very familiar with the rigors of training and the electric prod, though they escaped being wetted down when shocked. They showed her their scars from the burns; they said the pain when the volts charged through their bodies was like no other. Alberta had nightmares on and off for many months and still does every now and then. I tried to comprehend the mental anguish Little Andy experienced, with all four legs chained and after being wetted down with a hose, knowing 220 volts of electricity was coming and he could not get away. Poor Little Andy, may he rest in peace.

***

Yogi and BooBoo had not stopped eating since they arrived at the forest, and it did not take long for them to start to fill out. After six months, each gained almost a thousand pounds. Upon release to our side of the forest, extremely shy and scared, they huddled together, trunks entwined. Hank and I welcomed and befriended them. They really were extremely cute. I remembered at their age, I lived with Frankie at the zoo. Oh Frankie, I so wished him here. I know he would have been kind to these little guys and helped them adjust.

"Hello, my name is Ernest," I said, extending my trunk. "Do not be afraid. Hank and I want to be your friends."

They shyly extended their trunks to each of us. The vast open spaces overwhelmed them. Their entire lives thus far had been spent in a desolate cement cell in an extremely cold climate. They arrived at the zoo around the same time, both of them close to three years old. Devastated and missing their mothers, they only had each other. Neither one had ever seen a tree or mud or grass until they arrived at Bachelor's Forest. Hank and I introduced them to the wonders of mud.

Yogi and BooBoo shrieked with delight during their first mud-bath. Covered from head to toe, they rolled and rolled again all over the gigantic mud puddle. The next day we took them for a swim. Elephants are natural swimmers, and Yogi and BooBoo loved the water. We could not get them out after several hours, so Hank and I grazed while they swam, splashed, dunked, and howled with laughter. The joy on their little faces melted our hearts. Later that day, they stared wide-eyed as Hank and I stripped bark and knocked down a few trees. Every day for months, Hank and I introduced them to a new part of the forest, and every day they wallowed in the mud and swam.

One day, after our midmorning nap, the four of us were grazing on the hillside when Bart and Edward appeared out of nowhere. Yogi and BooBoo, enchanted and awed by Edward, followed him around the forest for the rest of the day and, as it would happen, for many years afterward. They loved him immediately. Hank resumed his daily wanderings with Bart and I sought out Owen and Oscar.

"The boys," as Alberta referred to them, had not left the fence since released from the holding area. Every day they stayed near Alberta and my mother, afraid to venture out. Hank and I invited them many times to join us on our outings, and they always refused. For some reason, that day, they accepted my offer.

22

THE BOYS

Animals are such agreeable friends – they ask no questions, they pass no criticisms.
—GEORGE ELLIOT

OWEN AND OSCAR were ages fourteen and fifteen, respectively. Little Andy, the youngest of the boys, had met his tragic end when only twelve years old. Owen and Oscar were deeply traumatized by his death, grief stricken and filled with guilt for not helping him. I remembered my powerlessness to help Maggie during our "breaking in" and told them so. We talked about everything. I shared the story about how I ended up at Bachelor's Forest. I told them about my beloved Maggie, Eve, and Frankie, as well as my reunion with my mother. They listened intently and, as time went on, they shared their stories.

Both were captive born and much too young when taken from their mothers. Oscar ended up at a zoo with an older female for about two years. She did not like Oscar and ignored him. In his loneliness, he fell into despondency. Inconsolable, he missed his mother terribly. Sad and lonely, he lost his will to live. He stopped eating. Taken from the zoo because his demeanor was bad for business, he went on the road for about five years, where he met Owen. He never performed, just traveled with the other elephants and used for elephant rides to draw preshow crowds. Oscar's friendship with Owen saved his life.

Owen, after taken from his mother, went immediately on the road. The other elephants—three females, Nancy, Jeanie, and Heather—had welcomed him with open hearts and helped him through the pain of missing his mother. They doted on and loved him completely. He lived on the road for six years and never performed. The company they traveled with went out of business. The females were sent to three different zoos and the boys ended up at the elephant rental company. Owen missed his surrogate mothers. He worried they might be terribly lonely without each other and was very sad at the thought he would never see them again.

Five years before coming to the forest, the boys met Alberta, Suzanna, and Izzie at the elephant rental company. The problem with male elephants is they can only be used in entertainment when young and small enough to be controlled. As they get older and grow bigger, they become difficult to control and considered too dangerous. This fact made it easy for Mr. William to bring them to Bachelor's Forest.

Both boys missed their friends from the road and were devastated at the news about Suzanna and Izzie. I felt bad for them and wondered if there would ever be an end to the pain of so much loss. I still deeply missed Eve and Frankie every day and hoped beyond hope my beloved Maggie had fallen into good hands.

***

FOR THE NEXT several months, the boys and I swam, wallowed in the mud, foraged, stripped bark, knocked down trees, dust-bathed, napped when tired, slept under the stars, or stayed up all night when we felt like it. Every morning, excited about another day of adventures, they began to look forward to whatever life offered each day. Their sadness waned and was replaced by bright eyes and happy smiles. As their confidence grew, we ventured farther into the forest. I remembered Eve telling me a captive elephant does not travel in a year what a wild elephant travels in a day. Some not even in their entire lives travel at all.

I had never journeyed into the forest without Hank or Edward before. Late one afternoon, after we plodded deep into the forest, I realized I did not know where we were. Do not panic, I told myself. Owen stretched to reach the top of a fig tree for its tender leaves. Oscar knocked down every tree he could. The sound of a small brook rippled nearby. We sought it out and enjoyed a refreshing drink from the cool water. Far off the beaten path, we could not find our way back from where we came. The boys, undaunted, tried many routes. We found lush vegetation, streams, birds, rabbits, and dense groupings of trees, but would we ever find our way out? Close to panic, it slowly dawned on me, it did not matter; we were on elephant time. We could wander around the forest forever. Where did we have to be? There were no humans waiting with sharp bull hooks or electric prods. The sun started to set and the frogs began their nightly noise. A few birds sang their lovely evening songs. Exhausted, we lay down to nap.

I awoke to a butterfly on the end of my trunk. I could see him clearly as the moonlight peeked through the treetops. I stood up and the butterfly landed on my head. I could feel his tiny feet walking about. I reached for him with my trunk. He flitted away. I knew when he landed on my head again because his tiny feet tickled. Hours later, the boys awakened ravenously hungry. We devoured the bark off several trees and continued our journey. As the sun became visible in the sky, the vibrant colors of the forest came alive and the birds chirped their break-of-day song. The crickets, now awake, joined in the music of sunrise. The boys skipped merrily along without a care in the world. The butterfly flitted along the path stopping now and then on a flower or tree branch.

The boys decided to follow him as he flitted between their trunks and mine. Their unadulterated glee began the passage to their elephantness. The butterfly crisscrossed, the boys skipped and laughed.

My heart swelled with happiness at their wild abandon and unselfconsciousness. The butterfly flew out of sight into a dense cluster of trees. The boys, determined to continue their little game, pushed right through the trees. I followed. We crashed through the trees to the other side where the butterfly flitted about an open area where Hank and Bart grazed. Edward, accompanied by Yogi and BooBoo, stood at the highest peak of the forest, his usual majestic presence commanding awe as he scanned the valley below.

The boys trumpeted and ran after the butterfly across the field as it flitted about, making figure eights. He landed on a fence post near my mother, Alberta, Anna, and Edna as they grazed. Portia and Calpurnia, covered from head to toe, enjoyed their daily mudbath. When we reached the fence the butterfly landed on the tip of my trunk, and then flew away.

23

HELLO, OLD FRIEND

One sees clearly only with the heart. Anything
essential is invisible to the eyes.
—ANTOINE DE SAINT-EXUPÉRY

MY FOURTH YEAR at Bachelor's Forest, in the early spring,
I experienced a surge of testosterone again. Bart
laughed at me while everyone else ignored me. The
entire population of the forest stayed as far away from
me as possible. Miserable, I could not eat. I could not
sleep. During this phase in the wee hours of the morning, the only one awake, I felt the vibrations of a big
truck. In the middle of the night? I wondered if I imagined the vibrations as I continued toward the barn. I
noticed my mother and Alberta headed slowly that way.
As I drew near, Edward was already well on his way.
Sure enough, within the hour, a big truck with eighteen
tires slowly headed up the road toward the barn.

This time I paced back and forth while Edward waited patiently. I had worn a path along the fence by the time the big truck arrived. The door opened and, as usual, out jumped Mr. William. I glanced at Edward, who continued to ignore me. My mother and Alberta averted their eyes when I glanced at them. A shrill trumpet blasted from the truck. My mother returned the trumpet with a louder blast. By now, everyone awake arrived to greet the newcomer. Another trumpet blast, louder this time. Again, my mother answered, much louder. Hay and bananas awaited the new arrival. Gentle Mr. William coaxed her out. As she slowly exited backward, another shrill trumpet blast, almost recognizable. My mother trumpeted many blasts, the new female almost completely out of the truck. The darkness made it difficult to see, but she appeared to have bloody bandages wrapped around her head. My mother trumpeted louder and louder and became more agitated, as did the newcomer. In my state of temporary insanity, I thought she resembled Eve. She looked like Eve but did not look like Eve. As Mr. William tenderly led her to the holding area, I realized bandages *were* wrapped around her head. My mother darted to the holding area, trumpeting her head off. From the other side of the holding area in the dark, I swore she looked like Eve. I roared her name. "Eve?" She trumpeted an answer.

I almost knocked Edward over as I ran toward Eve. My mother, already by her side, gently held her. Eve looked awful. "What happened?" I squeaked in horror.

My mother gave me *the look*. I hung back. Everyone kept a respectful distance while Eve stayed under the protective care of her dear friend, my mother. Mr. William tenderly changed her bandages. Not prepared to see what was under those bandages, my squeamishness made me turn away. Her skin hung off the side of her face in bloody chunks. One of her eyes was swollen shut; her left ear almost torn in half. She stood perfectly still while Mr. William cleaned and re-bandaged her wounds. She instinctively trusted him. Eve looked frail, too skinny—like Mary. I noticed her eye socket was sunken and her cheekbones pronounced as she savored banana after banana after banana.

My mother never left Eve's side for several months. She refused to leave and Mr. William allowed her to stay in the holding area while Eve healed. Eve may have looked like a broken, beaten-down elephant to all the onlookers, but her good eye still burned with such passion I knew she would survive. During the first few weeks, she ate nonstop. I am not sure she ever slept. Every time I saw her she was eating. In my agitated state, I maintained a respectful distance, but still kept an eye on how she was doing every day.

I noticed Edward paced a lot during Eve's initial rehabilitation. He too kept an eye on her, obviously concerned. We all were. We were confident between my mother and Mr. William she had the best care possible. Alberta trumpeted condolences from afar to her every day and she always trumpeted back her thanks. Calpurnia and Portia grazed nearby, available if needed. I watched them tenderly caress Eve's face to acknowledge her wounds and offer support. They visited daily, and I wondered what they talked about.

Mr. William watered a part of the area so Eve and my mother could mud-bathe. After a month, Eve began to lose her gaunt appearance, though still too thin, her skin more soft and supple from the mud as it hung loosely on her body. During this time Edward lumbered over to the fence and introduced himself to Eve. He gently touched her face and then her bandages with his trunk. She ran the end of her trunk softly all over his face, and then they hugged. They stood perfectly still, forehead to forehead for hours. My mother hung back respectfully. It was a magical moment forever etched in my memory. Two majestic old souls shared a mutual respect and understanding without ever speaking a word.

Later the same day, Edward dug up roots for Eve and my mother and hung around until Eve needed to rest. He visited with Eve and my mother every day, and soon Eve's bandages were removed for good. Her damaged eye lost its swollenness but she would never see out of it again. She began to look like herself once more. It was funny to hear her refer to my mother as "Stubbs." Nearly two months passed before I felt comfortable to come near enough to visit with Eve. I surprised myself when I started to cry as we hugged. "Oh Eve, you are safe now. It is going be all right. You are going to be all right. This is a magical place filled with other troubled souls who will help you heal. How I have missed you so!"

"This is as good as it gets in captivity," my mother rumbled softly.

Eve stared at me long and hard before she rumbled, "Ernest, you seem to have adjusted well without Maggie."

"I miss her every day," I answered, hanging my head sadly.

"I know Ernest, I know." She nodded and gave me one of those all-knowing Eve looks. I was ecstatic to be in her company again.

Three months passed before Eve was well enough to leave the holding area. Though scarred, her face healed nicely, and the blindness in her one eye did not deter her from exploring the forest. Her first day out, she and Edward on separate sides of the fence made the trek to the top of the highest hill. Eve moved slowly, as she had not exercised in many years. She may have been slow, but she was unstoppable. I stayed near the fence and watched her take in her new forever home. They stayed up on the hill, grazing all day, enjoying the warmth of the sun on their backs. I waited at the fence at dusk for them to return; they did not. Eve lay down for the first time since she arrived and slept under the stars. Edward stood guard beside his new friend.

The following morning, Eve joined the rest of us for breakfast. Edward accompanied her down the hill then trekked back to the top for some solitary time. He preferred to spend his time more alone than not. Yogi and BooBoo trailed him several feet behind. They adored him and followed him everywhere. Usually tolerant, he did not mind them hanging around; however, now and then he shooed them off. This was one of those days; he wanted to be alone. Yogi and BooBoo bounded back down the hill and joined the rest of us.

Calpurnia and Portia extended their trunks and warmly welcomed Eve to the forest. Edna and Anna, somewhat standoffish, nodded their welcomes. Alberta loved her instantly and followed her everywhere. My mother, Eve, and Alberta became an immediate and inseparable threesome. Impossible not to love Alberta, Eve's mothering instincts took over at once.

Eve learned her way around the forest quickly, because she had lots of guides. I remember the first time she, my mother, and Alberta ventured deep into the wooded area. I could hear her trumpets and squeals of delight as she ate bark and knocked down trees. How long had it been since she last played in the woods? My mother told me later, "Eve lay down and rubbed her back on the forest floor, legs in the air for what seemed like hours; then she scratched her back against the bark of the biggest tree she could find." They returned at dusk; Eve the giddiest I have ever seen her.

***

SEVERAL MONTHS AFTER Eve's recovery, while she was visiting with Edward one afternoon, my mother told Alberta and me what happened to her. Edward visited with Eve, just the two of them, a few times a week and I always wondered what those two kindred spirits talked about. Sometimes they pressed their foreheads together across the fence for quite some time. Other times they grazed quietly side by side. On those occasions they seemed to find strength in their mutual silence.

"About a year after you the left the zoo, Ernest, a new human, Mr. Chester, took over the care of the elephants. Unwise to the ways of elephants, he bullied them all. He called Eve "Beady" because she had beady little eyes. Of course, Eve did not respond when he called her Beady. "My name is Eve," she'd rumble to him over and over. He decided to show her who was boss and withheld food. "Beady, Beady, Beady," he taunted. This went on for a year, Eve eating barely enough to stay alive. One day the head of the zoo witnessed Mr. Chester's behavior and fired him on the spot. The next day a new human appeared. I didn't catch his name. He insisted Eve and the others stand at attention for hours. If they even blinked, he whacked them with his bull hook. One of the elephants defecated during one of these drills and the human stuck and twisted the pointy end of the bull hook in her anus so hard she screamed and fell to the ground. Eve grabbed him with her trunk and hurled him in the air. Dead before he ever hit the ground, he died from a heart attack. The wounded elephant had to be euthanized because the damage was unfixable. Eve, now a dangerous elephant, was shackled and put in solitary confinement for two years!"

I did not want to hear any more. Poor Eve!

"The other elephant, Donna, had enough of yet another new human and grabbed the bull hook out of his hand and hit him over the head. He died instantly. The zoo closed its elephant exhibit to the public. While the zoo tried to figure out what to do with the elephants, Eve and Donna stayed temporarily under the care of Mr. Skipper."

"Mr. Skipper? The same Mr. Skipper?"

"Yes, she had met him before, with you, years ago. He freed Eve from her shackles and cleaned her up. She was so stiff she could hardly walk. He uncontaminated her, she was so filthy."

I remembered how filthy I was when Mr. William found me. I'd been standing in my own excrement for six months. I could not imagine two years in shackles, standing in excrement.

"Eve and Donna had it pretty good for several months under the care of Mr. Skipper. Eve told me she walked around the small enclosure all day long. She kept moving because she could. Her feet and legs hurt from standing in one place for so long."

"Two years!"

"Almost six months ago, after the zoo closed for the day, Mr. Chester broke in to settle the score with Eve. Apparently he blamed her for being fired."

I failed to see the connection. "Humans!" I could hear Frankie grumble.

"He shackled her two front legs together, and then smacked her in the face with an ax handle. I believe that blow caused the blindness. On her knees, he hit the side of her face with the ax handle until she was a bloody pulp. Donna, sound asleep, woke to Eve's screams. She knocked him down with her trunk and stepped on his head. Then she trumpeted for hours, calling for help as Eve lay on her side, bleeding. That is how Mr. Skipper found her the next morning.

"Mr. Skipper immediately called the vet and then called Mr. William. Mr. William arrived less than a day later after driving nonstop for twenty hours. Eve does not know what happened to Donna."

Stunned, I glanced at my mother, and then at Alberta, who cried and cried.

***

I REMEMBER THE day Eve officially met Hank. I was almost twenty-five when Eve arrived at the forest. Hank, at sixteen, was almost the same size as me. Hank the Tank, as solid as they came, looked older than his years due to his size. He still had a baby face though. I introduced them one rainy afternoon shortly after Eve left the holding area. Hank fell in love with Eve in about two seconds. She had a way about her that made anyone she came into contact feel safe and special. Majestic Eve, my wise and intuitive friend, looked deep into Hank's eyes and saw his soul. And he knew it. It was impossible to hide from Eve; she saw everything. I believe we all want to be seen as we really are, though captivity often makes it difficult to *be* who we truly are. Hank spent time with Eve almost every single day. Although we males at the forest enjoyed our solitude as we would in the wild, oddly, we spent much of our time with our female friends and surrogate family unlike male elephants in the wild.

Bart remained standoffish in his typical Bart way for quite some time. He had the hardest time with change, wanting things to stay as they were. He needed predictability; it made him feel safe. Eve sensed that about Bart, and allowed things to progress on Bart time.

The boys, off doing their own thing, were practically unaware someone new had arrived. They behaved the most wild of any of us, and spent hardly any time with the females. I felt sorry for them when they experienced their heightened surge of testosterone as there were no receptive females. None of the ladies at the forest were interested in breeding at all—including Alberta, who was still much too young.

***

I FOUND IT interesting the way our lives began to fit together. My mother and Eve said our natural behaviors were now finally able to surface, allowing us to adapt to the ebb and flow of elephant life. Calpurnia and Portia, though still part of the family, preferred to live on the fringe of the female group. Eve, my mother, and Alberta—a tight group—became the core as Eve naturally stepped into the role of matriarch. Anna and Edna, not up to the task, were happy to finally have a leader. Calpurnia and Portia checked in several times a day and were never completely out of sight. The females actually lived and functioned similar to a wild herd. They traveled the forest loosely together. Rarely did twosomes go off by themselves, and if they did, they always checked in on a daily basis. It did not happen all at once, yet as each individual female came into her own elephantness, the group created its own elephant society. This was quite a remarkable feat considering they had spent the better parts of their lives in captivity, unable to be themselves, to truly be elephants.

The males resembled the loose-knit bachelor herds of the wild, though a few of us enjoyed spending nonbreeding time with the females. I make no apologies or excuses for wanting to spend time with my mother and Eve; we were making up for lost time. Hank too loved the company of my mother and Eve and spent an unusual amount of time with them. Calpurnia and Portia tolerated me and Hank. Edna and Anna tolerated us less. They acted completely different when Edward showed up, though. I think all the ladies had a secret crush on him. Whenever he came to visit his good friend Eve, they all swooned.

Bart and the boys rarely came around the ladies and spent most of their time deep in the forest, where they found a clearing and sunbathed and wallowed in a shallow pond. They still climbed up the hill several times a week to take in the grandeur of their forever home, always on the periphery of the females, nonchalantly checking in now and then. Yogi and BooBoo followed Bart and the boys into the woods on the days when Edward wanted to be left on his own. We all looked out for one another, each in our own way.

We kept an eye on each other's whereabouts and checked in every few days; it was important to our well-being to know everyone was safe.

***

THE YEARS PASSED quickly, and I often wondered why no new elephants came to the forest. I remember the year I turned thirty; by then our lives were routine, safe, and worry-free. Even so, I found myself worrying about all the other elephants, out in the world of humans, who would never make it to the forest. Eve, at fifty-nine, was more majestic than ever. Edward, about fifty-seven (though none of us were sure of his exact age), continued his almost daily visits with her. My mother was even more beautiful and serene at fifty, and Alberta blossomed into a very beautiful and high-spirited eighteen-year-old.

The boys, now twenty-three and twenty-four, were huge, weighing about five and a half tons each. Yogi and BooBoo, at fifteen, were not far behind at four and four and a half tons, respectively. Inseparable, both extremely handsome young bulls, they still loved to hang out with Edward as often as he allowed it. Bart had mellowed tremendously, and at thirty-five was coming into his own. He began to spend more of his time with Eve. He weighed almost six tons, and Hank no longer let him win at wrestling. Bart had developed an air of quiet confidence. Hank now twenty-two, weighed not quite six tons, and looked more like a tank than ever. He still had a crush on Alberta, though she did not return his affection. He did not mind, he felt happy just to be in her company. Anna, the seasoned master at stealing our bananas, never told any of us her age. Even Edna, the sweetest elephant and still enormous at forty-three years old, did not know her good friend's age. Calpurnia and Portia were well into their fifties, and probably even pushing sixty, though they never admitted their ages even when we all tried to guess one afternoon.

All survivors, we became a family. A *dysfunctional* family, as Eve would say. A sense of community made us all feel like we belonged. For so many years without a sense of family, we felt lost. After ten years in the forest, I loved them all—everyone differently, but love it was. Eve and my mother taught me how love is in each of us, though it is hard to find when fear grabs hold of us. Love will outlive us all. It is what we leave behind after everything else fades away, and why Frankie still lives on. But love goes beyond memory. His love lives inside me. It is hard to explain the changes love brought to the forest. Where fear once lived, love now resided. An elephant without other elephants is not an elephant!

I overheard Eve say to Edward one day, "Stubbs is right, better to live one day in the forest than forever in captivity. I finally found the peace my soul has longed for."

Edward silently nodded his agreement and rubbed his forehead against Eve's.

***

I REMEMBER WHEN Bart began his daily visits with Eve. He loved her like no other, and she taught him the wisdom of focusing on the good things in life. I can hear her say, "Sharing brings healing. Our shared burdens lighten our loads." I do not know the specifics of their conversations, but Bart became interested in the other elephants like never before. He reached out more. The same Bart, only better. Battered and scarred, traded like furniture in the world of thoughtless humans, for a long time he shuffled along, listless, hurt, and angry. And that was exactly how Mr. William found him. I do not understand the motives of the human heart. I do know that facing our fears while living in Bachelor's Forest was easy compared to the years we had all spent feeling helpless, inadequate, dependent, and hopeless. Whatever losses Bart experienced, he only shared with Edward and Eve.

One afternoon, I overheard Eve comforting Bart. "We are here to comfort each other when in need," she said. "Here the brokenhearted heal. There is a time to cry. Our grief has drained us. We need rest. Here we can heal and rest. We live in a peaceful place, undisturbed by humans. Our past hectic lives exhausted us. Let's be thankful for the quiet times in our present peaceful place where we can be renewed."

We socialized, ate, drank, exercised, rested, socialized, ate, drank, exercised, rested, and repeated the pattern every day. Gentle Eve exuded patience, kindness, goodness, joy, peace, and—most of all—love.

She lovingly rumbled to us, "We must mourn our wounds and our losses so we can move on to live fully in the present."

The days flew by as all things began to feel familiar. There exists a knowingness I cannot put into words. We delighted in our connection to each other, the forest, and our newfound elephant society. We knew intuitively we belonged to something much larger than ourselves. It felt good to be alive.

As we bonded and became an elephant family, I began to truly understand how important it was for Frankie to remember his family and his life in the wild. His memory of them and their love kept him from going insane. Now, as part of an elephant society and living as a family, when I imagined his old life, I could actually comprehend his love for his family and just how much he desperately missed them. He ended up in a strange land, far, far away from his home and all he knew, yet his dreams must have seemed so real he could have almost touched them. He thought he could bend the entire universe with the force of his will and see his family again. If only he could have. At times, they seemed so close he could almost grab hold of them. Yet each day they eluded him, so with every tomorrow he ran faster, trunk stretched out farther, his huge heart breaking, only to dream again another day. When he finally grasped he would *never* see his family again and his dreams were already behind him, far away across the ocean in the vast shadows of his memory, he lost his resolve to live and lay down to die. I wished with all my heart and soul I could will him to the forest with me. I still miss him every single day. Oh Frankie, how did you stand it?

24

A ONCE-IN-A-LIFETIME FRIEND

*Love recognizes no barriers. It
jumps hurdles, leaps fences,
penetrates walls to arrive at its destination full of hope.*
—MAYA ANGELOU

TWO EVENTS OCCURRED in my thirty-fifth year that forever changed my life. The first happened in early spring. Late one afternoon, the sun finally peeked out from behind the clouds after many days of nonstop rain. Hank and I fed on the fresh, lush, green grass by the fence near my mother and Eve. So enjoying the moment, we did not feel the vibrations of the big truck approaching until it was so close we actually heard it. Eve looked up first, then me, then my mom and Hank. We looked at each other knowingly, excited and apprehensive about our yet unknown comrade.

"Here we go again," trumpeted Eve.

It had been a long time and was always bitter-sweet when a new arrival finally made it to the forest after years of heartache, cruelty, and abuse beyond comprehension. We knew all too well the long healing process and we are always sad to hear the newcomers' tales. But heal we did and we were always ready to do whatever it took to help each other along.

The four of us walked along the fence toward the gate to welcome whoever was on the truck. As had been our tradition, we would all be present to welcome any new arrivals. The truck pulled into the front of the barn as we rounded the bend. My mother and Eve arrived before Hank and me, as we had to travel an extra loop to get to the other side of the truck. Bart and Edward waited patiently, and we came up the side yard at the same time as the rest of the ladies. Our new friends had already backed out of the truck as a female human coaxed them. I stared at the human for a few seconds and recognized her instantly! I was about to trumpet a greeting when I turned my attention to the new arrivals, a mother and a very young male of no more than two or three. The mother seemed confused, uncertain. Rather overweight, maybe 500 to 1,000 pounds, and from the side she looked to be a little younger than me, maybe in her mid-thirties. She snorted and rumbled uneasily. Eve and my mother extended their trunks in greeting. She did not accept their greeting, and as she turned away from them, I found myself staring at a most beautiful elephant, with big floppy ears and an unusually short trunk.

I tripped over myself onto my knees as the glands on my face began secreting. I then peed all over myself and trumpeted maniacally, unable to control myself. I bellowed, I rumbled, I growled, I roared. I trumpeted so loud the tops of the trees shook. A worried Hank ran over and helped me to my feet. My mother and Eve stared at me, obviously concerned. I could not breathe. My heart stuck in my throat. I ran to the fence in a blur, tears falling down my face. I could not stop crying, and my heart pounded so hard; the pounding was all I could hear, my heart almost burst out of my chest. The new arrival turned to see what all the commotion was about, then locked her eyes on my face and froze. She fell to her knees and bellowed, growled, roared, rumbled, and trumpeted the longest most soulful trumpet I have ever heard in my life. The air still vibrated waves of sound for minutes after she finished. She too cried, and peed all over herself; her face glands secreted more than mine. The alarmed humans moved behind a protective barrier. Eve and my mother grabbed the youngster, who stood terrified amid the uproar. More trumpet blasts, louder than the last. We kept up a fit of roaring for a good ten minutes. Could it be so? I was unable to get to her; the steel fence separated us. Ears flapping wildly, I rammed my massive body into it again and again as she wobbled toward me as fast as she could. We leaned into the fence desperate to get to one another, we hugged each other as tears streamed down our faces, trunks all over each other; the rest of the world did not exist. Here was my beloved Maggie!

My mother told me later when everyone realized it was Maggie, the cacophony of trumpets was so loud the humans covered their ears and the buildings shook. "All of us elephants were crying tears for you two; even the humans were crying! You were both oblivious to the world around you, and what a spectacle you made!"

With an incredible display of strength that surprised us both, the steel fence now lay flat on the ground, a feat supposedly impossible. Nothing could have prepared me for the surge of emotion that overcame me when I first saw my beautiful Maggie's sweet face.

We stayed outside all night. Trunks entwined, we gently hugged under an almost full moon. We cried, we laughed, and cried again until the sun came up.

"Ernest, you look exactly the same, only bigger! I would recognize you anywhere. You are still very handsome, the handsomest elephant ever!" she cried tearfully as she batted those beautiful eyelashes at me. "Riding away that day thinking I would never see you again was the saddest day of my life!"

"Oh Maggie, you are a sight for sore eyes." And she was. "Still the most beautiful elephant I have ever laid eyes on!" I did not say anything about her weight because I would never hurt her feelings, and besides, it did not take away from her beauty. She was still very beautiful indeed! "Where have you been for the past twenty years? Never a day went by I did not think of you and wonder how and where you were and what kind of human you ended up with!"

Come to find out when we separated all those years ago, Maggie and Ms. Hope went to a zoo, where Maggie remained a solitary elephant for eighteen of the twenty years since I last saw her. She was transferred to a breeding facility four years ago, where she gave birth to a little boy, and then was sent back to the lonely barren zoo.

"What is your son's name?"

"Ernest."

My heart leapt into my throat.

"I call him little Ernie but he will be Ernest when he grows up."

There were no words. It took weeks for my heart to beat normally and for me to completely catch my breath. How can I explain the pain and the joy I felt seeing her again after all those years? We will forever share a silent bond that only survivors who have suffered together share. Those who have never suffered with another will not and cannot understand that bond. We stayed awake until morning; sleep was impossible. So intense our connection our hearts seemed to beat as one elephant. I breathed in her essence, feeling her skin, and touching her face, consumed by her. We hugged with our trunks entwined, told our stories, and took turns weeping. We laughed as we shared our hopes, our dreams, and our joys. We shared our pain and heartaches and wept together.

"The freezing winters and sweltering summers at the zoo reminded me of the boxcars when we lived on the road," she said. "I spent most of the winters inside the most barren and fruitless place on earth, my desolate cement prison, too cold to venture out. And the monotony, the clamor, the noise, the coming and going of strangers, the eternal procession of whiny little human children. I became agitated and restless; I faced the future with hopeless dread.

"I could only smell cement day in and day out; wet cement, dry cement, cold cement, hot cement. I thought I would lose my mind, and I was so bored I cried all the time.

"At the zoo, the bleak outside enclosure had no trees, no bushes, no dirt for dusting, no mud for wallowing, no pool, and no area for browsing, though Ms. Hope did her best to ensure I had fresh hay every day and lots of bananas. I missed you and Eve terribly and ached with loneliness, the pain suffocating at times. My memories of you and Eve kept me going some. Ms. Hope played with me every day, and that helped a little. I slept a lot. I became fat and lazy with nothing to do but stand around, sleep, and eat.

"The cement is not kind to our feet and joints like the giving earth. At the breeding facility I stood on a hard surface, unable to move, chained sixteen hours a day. My life was so hollow I did not recognize myself. Ms. Hope walked me when she noticed I was especially disheartened. She could feel my hopelessness.

"The thought of Ernie spending his life in desolation caused me many sleepless nights. One day when Ernie looked at me, I saw myself as he saw me. It made me love him even more than I thought possible. I saw myself again. I ran over to Ms. Hope and put my trunk in her hand and I gazed into her eyes, pleading for her to get us out of there. She understood."

Ms. Hope heard about Bachelor's Forest and contacted Mr. William, who had offered her a job. Ms. Hope walked Maggie and little Ernie out of the zoo one night and brought them to the forest two days later. What a relief to know gentle Ms. Hope took care of my sweet Maggie the entire time we had been apart, including the two years Maggie spent at the breeding facility.

***

WELL, IMAGINE THE commotion from the others as we ventured up the hill the next morning for breakfast. Little Ernie, in the care of Eve and my mother, loudly bellowed his disapproval of his mother staying out all night as he darted over to Maggie and voraciously suckled. I recognized Ms. Hope immediately. The years had treated her kindly; she looked exactly the same except for a few extra pounds, like Maggie. I rumbled a greeting and extended my trunk to her. She reached for and held my trunk.

"My goodness Ernest, what a gorgeous bull you are! And such a big boy! You must weigh at least six tons! You are so big and handsome!" She hugged my trunk. Maggie butted in and grabbed my trunk with hers, gently nudging Ms. Hope away from me as Little Ernie hung on tight and suckled to his heart's content. My beloved Maggie was home at last.

***

MAGGIE CRIED EVERY day for several weeks. Every time she looked at Ernie, tears flowed down her sweet face. She visited me by the fence and her eyes welled up as she chewed the delicious fresh grass and the roots I dug up for her. She cried when she reunited with Eve, and sobbed uncontrollably when she learned of my reunion with my mother. She cried when she met my mother, who gently caressed her face, eyes, ears, and mouth after Maggie extended her trunk in greeting. She adored Maggie immediately. So did Alberta, who fell madly in love with little Ernie. Anna and Edna, utterly enamored with Maggie, competed with my mother and Eve for her attention. Calpurnia and Portia were curious about the newcomer, but kept a respectful distance and watched with detached interest. Little Ernie was concerned about his mother, and nuzzled her whenever she cried. She explained to him they were happy tears. Sometimes when Ernie napped, Maggie and I quietly wept side by side at the fence, unable to find words to express our joy and happiness.

***

AS THE NIGHTS grew warmer, Maggie and Ernie slept under a blanket of stars simply because they could. During the days, Ernie watched in awe as we knocked over trees, dug up roots, stripped bark, threw dust on our backs with our trunks, napped, and mud-bathed. The first time Ernie attempted a dust bath, dirt went everywhere because he completely missed his back.

A bit embarrassed, he dropped to the ground and rolled in the dirt, his little legs waving in the air. When he stood up again, Eve patiently showed him how to use his trunk. After a few more tries, Ernie was completely covered in dirt, as was everyone within trunk distance, and we applauded with squeaks, chirps, and loud trumpets.

Enormous Edna could not keep her trunk off little Ernie. He stood perfectly still, not pulling away when Edna nuzzled him. Instead he contentedly flapped his big ears and gently touched her with his short trunk. After our late morning feast, the ladies lumbered out to mud-wallow. Ernie followed, though lagging behind a little. My mother backtracked and approached Ernie, who stopped walking when she reached out and gently touched him with her trunk. I watched him reach out a little shyly at first. In a few minutes they both headed out across the field, trunks entwined, his big ears flapping as they disappeared over a small hill to join the others.

Ernie had never played in mud. In fact, he had never even seen mud before. My mother told me how he stared in wonder as Enormous Edna and Anna Banana mud-wallowed and dunked each other in the pond. At first he did not go in the mud. He just enjoyed scanning the area and observing the others strip bark from the trees. Maggie told me he had never seen a tree before! He observed Eve and my mother graze, and decided to do the same. All of his life when he was not suckling, he drank water out of a bucket and had eaten only an occasional square of hay.

All he needed was for us to show him what to do, though, and before long Ernie became proficient at foraging, dust-bathing, swimming, and breaking branches off trees to cram into his mouth. The first time Ernie swam, so intense was his enjoyment it brought tears to my eyes. I looked at Maggie, who acknowledged my memory with a smile. The first time I swam had been with her. That seemed so long ago, in a land far away. Edna and Anna took turns squirting Ernie with their trunks. He squealed delightedly. We all shared in his excitement with gleeful chirps, rumbles, squeaks, and bellows.

After their mud-bath, all the ladies had to inspect Ernie from head to toe with their trunks. He had been hesitant at first, but it became almost impossible to keep Ernie out of the mud once he finally learned the wonders of mud on elephant skin. Alberta nudged him into the mud the first time then nudged him out when it was time to go. Though he seemed to enjoy attention from all the ladies, my mother and little Ernie became the best of friends. He was the same age as me when I was taken from her. I could tell she loved him; she was never able to get enough of him. She must have felt young again enjoying the role of doting aunt. At thirty-five years old, I was too old for her to mother me. He did not know he was about to be adopted by seven wannabe moms. It had been a long while since any of them had been around a baby, if at all. And who could resist those eyelashes? They were all eager to use their latent mothering skills.

It did not take little Ernie long to become the beloved child of Bachelor's Forest. I do not think he realized his impact on all of us; his very presence helped heal many shattered lives. His sweet innocence and childlike trust helped dissipate the subtle cloud of ever-present sadness. His big ears, undersized trunk, wiggly little body and beautiful bright eyes brought us all tremendous joy. Here was a fresh new life untainted by the dark side of humanity.

How we loved Ernie's naughty ways! He learned from the master, and soon made it a game to snatch Anna's bananas. Of course, he never ate them. He became quite adept at stealing them before she knew they were gone. She roared her displeasure and scolded Ernie good-naturedly most of the time. Sometimes she tried to shame him for taking an old lady's food. He always acted remorseful; his head hung low and his trunk dragging on the ground as we all watched in amusement.

He loved to sneak up behind us and pull our tails. It never hurt, just startled and annoyed us. His favorite game was to steal the food right out of our mouths! Greatly excited and making little squeals and rumbles of pleasure he stuck his trunk right in our mouths and sampled our food. None of us minded though.

***

MY MOTHER, EVE, Alberta, and now Maggie were inseparable, the best of friends. I must admit I always felt a little jealous and left out and I wondered what they talked about. It was "girl talk", according to Maggie, perhaps just old friends catching up. I know how much Maggie and Eve adored each other. Of course, I wondered if they ever talked about me. During these girl talks I spent a lot of time with Edward, Bart, and Hank. Yogi, BooBoo, and Bart had a really big crush on Maggie. Actually, we all did! Bart's crush was obvious because he became speechless and clumsy when in her presence. Yogi and BooBoo's crush even more obvious as they competed outwardly for her attention by being show-offs.

Ernie enjoyed his time hanging out with the guys. He reached through the fence and, just as with the ladies, stole the food right out of our mouths. Ernie was captivated by Edward; upon first meeting him he stared deep into his sad wrinkled face and immediately recognized the individual living deep inside. He seemed to sense the horror Edward had endured that no words could describe. His little heart burst with compassion, and he immediately loved Edward. He hugged Edward every single day several times a day without saying a word. He still does. And Edward silently hugs him back.

**

IT WAS HEARTWARMING to witness Ernie's reaction to birds gliding through the treetops. He screeched with happiness and wonder as their voices echoed in the brilliant sky. Maggie shared with me their reaction the first time they saw their reflections in the pond.

"We stood on the bank of the pond and little Ernie looked out from the water." Maggie batted her beautiful eyelashes at me and continued, "How strange, I thought, as I did not see him enter the pond. I looked up and there he stood beside me. I quickly looked back at the water and there he was! How could he be in two places at once? Well you should have seen Ernie when he thought I was in the water. Trumpet after trumpet blast, he called for me to come out. When he saw me standing next to him it startled him so much, he somersaulted into the pond. He splashed about as he tried to get his bearings. He finally climbed up the bank, trumpeting his confusion. We both stared into the pond and saw ourselves staring back from the water! No matter which way I moved my trunk, the elephant in the water did so exactly. Ernie shrieked when he realized the elephant in the water was his reflection. I must say, I had never seen myself, and was quite surprised to see a mature elephant looking back. I still think of myself as young. Where do the years go, Ernest?"

Ernie gathered sticks, leaves, and twigs into a pile as we visited. He then proceeded to dust-bathe. His aim still needed a little work, and dirt flew everywhere.

Maggie smiled at Ernie and the mess he made. She asked me if it was possible to love him more than she did at that moment. Maggie loved Ernie with every ounce of her being, which was considerable at 9,000 pounds.

A crash of thunder and all of a sudden the rain started to come down hard. The others headed back to the barn while Maggie, Edward, and I took shelter under the tree. Hank ran ahead for his usual cover. Eve and Ernie remained out in the open meadow, with not even a tree to shelter them. Ernie stood in the downpour and cried; his sweet little face pure joy. They looked to the sky, and not even the thunder deterred them, so precious was the moment. Anna and Edna looked over their shoulders and smiled knowingly at each other. Ernie was coming into his own as an elephant. I could hear Eve and Ernie's gleeful laughter amid our trumpets and the thunder and the bliss of just being able to stand outside in the rain.

***

THERE COMES A point when a female elephant reaches her perfect time in life, when her face will never be as beautiful, her body never again as powerful or more graceful. It happened later that year to Maggie, though she had no idea how beautiful she was or the effect she had on others. She dropped almost 1,000 pounds, her legs strong from daily exercise, her skin supple and smooth from daily mud-baths. Her eyes were bright and her spirit at peace as she meandered through the rolling hills and lush vegetation. I often watched Maggie stop to throw dirt on her back to protect her sensitive skin against the bugs and the sun. Ernie would do the same as he stood quietly by her side. The birds sang in the treetops and the bright sun smiled down on creation's masterpiece. All living things have their hour in the sun and this was indeed Maggie's time to bloom.

***

LATER THAT FALL, I spent all day in the forest with Hank, Yogi, and BooBoo, who Edward had shooed away earlier that morning. We ran into Owen and Oscar, who I had not seen in a while. I was always relieved to know they were OK. We followed them to the clearing with a large pool of mud as the brilliant sun warmed the chilly air. We spent most of the day immersed in the cool mud. Afterward we grazed our way out of the forest as the sun faded from the sky. I met my mother at the fence who looked more tired than usual. She seemed to be slowing down some. Edward and Bart competed for Eve's attention. Maggie, Ernie, and Alberta napped on the hillside, while Anna and Edna grazed close by. Yogi and BooBoo ran trumpeting to greet my mother and Eve like two long-lost friends even though they had just seen them that morning. Hank, the last to arrive at the fence, stopped and visited with Calpurnia and Portia before saying good night to Eve and my mother.

Tired from the day's festivities, my mother and I visited awhile. "That Ernie is something else," she said, smiling as her eyes twinkled. "He reminds me of you, always in motion and curious about everything. He wears me out. He is never out of sight of his mother. Maggie keeps a good eye on him. He seems scared to venture too far from her. Oh, Ernest, you were the sweetest child! I thought I would die the day they took you from me."

I saw the pain on her face. "I suffered without you too, Mom." I touched her face with my trunk. "I missed you every single day."

We stayed close, our heads touching for a long time until, exhausted, we said good night. She retired to the barn because she tolerated the cold less and less as she got older.

I slept hard after my mother left. So hard I never heard Maggie and Ernie arrive for our morning breakfast together. Ernie stuck his little trunk in my mouth to wake me. As I grumbled, he squeaked out a shrill trumpet. I awoke with a start. I was dreaming of Frankie and me at the cement prison. When I opened my eyes, little Ernie stood staring at me. I looked up to see Maggie smiling at him, the proud mother. I stood up just as Eve, my mom, and Edna joined us. As I wondered the whereabouts of Hank and Bart, they snuck up behind me and made me jump. Edward, Yogi, and BooBoo grazed nearby. The rest of the girls had already been awake for hours and, full from breakfast, enjoyed a warm mud-bath under the intense heat of the sun, though the air was very cool.

Ernie pulled Edna's, then my mother's, and then Eve's tail as he ran circles around them. Where did he get his energy? In the eight months he lived at the forest he gained almost 1,000 pounds while his mother lost almost the same amount of weight. We all looked forward to another day with Ernie. Yogi and BooBoo, curious about the little guy, reached through the fence with their trunks. He extended his trunk in greeting, but not before he gave Edward his daily hug. Ernie reached into Yogi and BooBoo's mouths for food. Disappointed, he moved to a huge pile of bananas that lay nearby. We joined him and feasted on bananas for most of the morning.

Hank, Edward, and I climbed our favorite hill as Bart, Yogi, and BooBoo joined the boys deep in the bowels of the woodlands.

We reached the top of the hill and stood high above the valley below. I felt humbled by the greatness and power of the universe. Like the highest eagle, I soared, circling. I breathed in the pure clean air and again observed creation's masterpiece. The bright gold, red, orange, and yellow leaves of autumn blazed across the floor of the valley below me. I took it all in and could not help but feel deeply moved. Overwhelmed with gratitude and awe, my wounds and my worries disappeared. The three great loves of my life grazed happily below and I felt indebted to them for filling my life with love and meaning. Without them I would be painfully lonely and terribly alone. An enduring sense of love and appreciation for all that is good in the world washed over me. I knew how lucky we were to have a second chance to live the lives that were taken from us. I took another deep breath of the fresh clean air and in my thankfulness and wonder, my heart opened and my soul could not help but sing. Hank and Edward must have felt it too. It would be difficult not to.

***

TIME IS A funny thing. The days, weeks, months, and years melted one into another. Time passed much too quickly living in the forest. Yet while at the cement prison with Frankie, time went by slowly, each day excruciatingly and painfully long. I looked back at my time on the road, and it seemed more like one long horrible nightmare from which I could not wake up. Yet the fifteen years I had now lived with my mother in the forest had flown by, a blur.

One late winter morning she did not come to the fence for breakfast, and I was disappointed because every day I looked forward to her joyful morning greeting. Maggie and Ernie, concerned, went to the barn to check on her. Hank and I paced nervously by the fence. After what seemed like forever, the three of them appeared. My mother, sound asleep, had not heard them enter. Ernie had gone to my mother and awakened her in his typical fashion, sticking his trunk in her mouth.

"I dreamed of your father," my mother rumbled softly as she stared into my face. "I did not want to wake up; I have not dreamed of him in a very long time."

I could not help but notice how tired she looked. Hank noticed too. Eve and Maggie stood on either side of her as she ate some bananas. Hank and I stayed close to the ladies for the rest of the day to keep an eye on her. She seemed fine as she grazed with the others for the rest of the morning. She lay down on the hill with Eve as Maggie stood nearby with Ernie for several hours. Not interested in a mud-bath, she grazed as the others wallowed in the cool mud for hours. By dinnertime she seemed fine as we all lingered near the fence. She visited with Edward, Hank, and me before she returned to the barn a little earlier than usual, causing Hank to pace. Edward suggested we not worry; my mother knew how to take care of herself. The three of us stayed up later than usual under a blanket of stars. Everyone else was sound asleep. Eve, Maggie, Alberta, and Ernie slept in the barn that night. Edward shared a story about Bart with Hank and me that night that I will never forget.

"As a very young elephant, Bart was trained to give rides at an amusement park. Zeus, a little older than him and quite the hellion, had a history of aggression toward the humans. As we know, bull elephants are more aggressive than females. The violent and cruel training we endure as young bulls is an attempt to keep us manageable enough to be used for breeding when we get older." Edward paused at the thought. "After several episodes at the park where they lived, Zeus went under the control of a well-known 'elephant boss' who specialized in training elephants for rides. Zeus refused to perform a command and attempted to flee the training tent. Bart heard him scream in pain, and then saw the human repeatedly stab him with the sharp end of the bull hook. Blood gushed out of the puncture wounds on his leg as he attempted to crawl away. Humans chain unruly elephants to incapacitate them. They chained Zeus and he could barely move. For most of the summer he had no shade or shelter, and they fed him minimal food. The humans gave him water so infrequently his physical strength declined. Still undaunted by electric shock, he refused to give in. Determined to subdue him, one of the humans rammed Zeus with a bulldozer to show him who was boss! They rammed him several times in the back and twice in the head as he lay on the ground, chained, with his legs uncomfortably outstretched. They left him laying there, the skin on the top of his head flapped open to a bloody pulp! He could not stand up because he was so damaged by his injuries. This made it impossible to move him, so the humans euthanized him after he suffered in agony for two months. For *two months* he lay there in unspeakable pain! Chained and powerless to help, it was torture for Bart to watch his suffering day after day. He rumbled to him every day how sorry he felt. Tears of pain and sorrow trickled down Zeus's cheeks. He died a long, drawn-out, and excruciatingly painful death, a dark and terrible experience." Edward shuddered and hung his head. He closed his eyes. "Rest in peace, my friend."

Hank and I, stunned, exchanged glances. We were too horrified to speak. Poor Zeus. Poor Bart! No wonder he never spoke of his past.

Hank and Edward slept a few hours, I not at all. I was worried about my mother and I could not get the horror of what happened to Zeus out of my mind. Proud Zeus would not succumb to the humiliating demands of the humans. They murdered his body but not his spirit. I wondered if he felt afraid as he took his last breath. I hoped not. I do not understand why humans enjoy harming another, nor can I comprehend the pleasure they receive from our pain. How savage, the nature of humankind! Humans demand we conform to their ways, but their ways are not our ways. I cannot imagine the wretchedness Zeus felt. The humans did not value him for who he was. I wondered what his life would have been like if he had never been captured. I could not get him out of my mind. I felt awful for Bart having to witness his friend's incomprehensible suffering. I remembered Frankie had told me how humans are the only species who kill for sport. "Good grief, they don't even eat what they kill! What a horrible waste of a life! At least the lion has enough respect to eat the antelope he just killed," he had snorted, flapping his ears indignantly.

Zeus died a horribly malicious death. His pride cost him his life. You are free, Zeus; you suffer no more at the hands of humankind.

Unable to sleep, I quietly walked to the fence right before dawn. Calpurnia and Portia joined me as the fiery orange sun slowly lit the landscape. The air chillier than usual, for winter had arrived. Bart, Yogi, and BooBoo joined Owen and Oscar in the forest that morning. Sweet Edna roared loudly at Anna for stealing her bananas. I guess she was hungrier than usual that morning. Edward and Hank quietly savored their own bananas. Ernie arrived in leaps and bounds from the barn. Alberta was next, devouring her bananas as if she had not eaten in days. Later than usual, my mother, followed by Eve and Maggie, went straight for the bananas. Hank and I sighed our mutual relief. Our anxiety lessened. Edward gently touched my mother's face with his trunk. She smiled sweetly causing the gray skin around her eyes to crinkle. Ernie sampled the food in all our mouths as we grazed. Edward and I dug up roots for my mother and Eve while Hank flirted with Alberta and Maggie.

Hank and I stayed in the company of my mother the rest of the day. Too cold for mud-bathing and too tired to forage, she preferred to stay close to the barn, and the three of us quietly enjoyed each other's company. Late in the afternoon, Ernie pulled my mother's tail and stole the food from her mouth before he ran off to hide behind his mother. I observed Eve and Edward at the top of the hill enjoying the comfort of one another.

The warm sun on my back made me sleepy. I lay down for a nap, followed by Hank, then my mother. We napped for hours and I dreamed of my mother and me when I was little. I dreamed I leaned against her sturdy body and felt her soft skin, listened to her strong heartbeat, and felt her warm breath on my face.

I awoke to a sunset of purples, pinks, and oranges as the temperature began to drop significantly. The clouds cleared, the stars twinkled between the bare branches, and the wind picked up a bit.

"We are too old to handle this cold weather. Plus, we are not designed for the cold. We are not polar bears. Good night!" Eve rumbled.

I watched as my mother and Eve slowly lumbered toward the barn, two old friends side by side. I remembered how much Mary hated the cold and the freezing train rides. Poor Mary, I hoped she was warm and comfortable, wherever she might be.

Edward, Hank, and I stayed in our barn that night—a rare occurrence indeed. We did not sleep, still worried about my mother. We warmed up quickly, and before long Yogi and BooBoo joined us. They huddled close to Hank and me for warmth and gazed at Edward adoringly. Bart and the boys stayed out in the woods all night.

The following morning, all of us were back outside as soon as the sun came up. Edward checked on my mother and then meandered to the top of the hill for some solitary time. Hank joined Yogi and BooBoo in the woods for most of the day. Alberta, who had stayed out all night with Edna and Anna, hummed as the sun warmed her back. Calpurnia and Portia spent the better part of the day in close proximity to my mother and Eve. Maggie and I hovered close to my mother the entire day as Ernie napped, played, ate, and then napped again.

"Your mother slept hard last night. She seems much better this morning," Maggie rumbled, her large ears flapping.

I glanced at my mother and Eve, when out of nowhere, a terrible sinking feeling overwhelmed me, a feeling we were all one body, one elephant, and if one of them disappeared, I would lose an important part of myself. "Are you all right?" Maggie stared at me concerned.

"I am afraid of losing my mother."

"Do not be afraid, Ernest, she lives inside you. Not even death can take away her love for you. Enjoy whatever time you have together. Our lives are but a blink in time."

"Ah my sweet Maggie, you are wise!"

Over to the fence I walked, and gently rubbed the tip of my trunk all over my mother's face. She sensed my concern and hugged and held me tight. We could not get enough of each other; Eve and Maggie exchanged knowing glances. I'm not sure how long my mother and I remained in our embrace, but I will remember that moment in time for the rest of my life, inhaling her essence with every breath I took and the feel of her soft wrinkly skin. My mother reminded me how much she loved me from the minute I was born. "You were even cuter than little Ernie," she whispered, and her face brightened. "Ernest, you will never know the pain I felt all those years without you. You brought joy to my heart and sunlight to my soul. Darkness set in after you were gone. Grief is the price we pay for love!"

After our evening meal, a few hours before sunset, she lay down to rest under the giant oak. Her breathing became labored as the sun began to disappear behind the tree tops. Eve, Maggie, Hank, and I stayed by her side until she took her last breath long after the sun went down. She was fifty-five years old. Little Ernie, too young to fully comprehend, stayed under the supervision of Edna and Anna several yards away. Portia and Calpurnia hovered close by. Edward began his descent down the hill the moment it happened. He

216

arrived in time to comfort Eve, who was devastated. Hank was inconsolable, and Maggie hugged me and held me for hours as I cried.

What a gift to spend that wonderful day together. I remember how the gray skin around my mother's beautiful, kind eyes crinkled as we laughed at Ernie's antics and her smile as she shared memories of my father. Embarrassed, she confessed she had a crush on Edward. Who knew? Hank, Maggie, and I were completely surprised. Eve said she had suspected from day one.

Rest in peace Clementine. You live forever in my heart.

***

I AM NOT sure who grieved most, Hank or me. Angry at having lost my mother again, I knocked down trees and bent the steel fence. I kicked the ground and accidently sent a cat in my path of destruction hurling through the air. He landed on his feet across the fence and glared at me. Hank lingered near my mother's grave everyday for weeks until her scent faded, committing her to his memory. How he loved her so. Utterly dejected, he lost all joy in living. Unable to comfort him, my own grief too unbearable, I spent the entire winter bereft and alone deep in the bowels of the forest. As I wallowed in my solitude, I thought a lot about Frankie. I could hear him say, "Good grief, Ernest, be thankful for the gift of the fifteen years you and your mother had together!" He was right. I know with all my heart that Frankie would have gladly given up his life to have one more day with his mother and family.

***

SPRING ARRIVED AND, as usual, everything came alive again. That included me and Hank. A dark night of the soul for both of us, he suffered terribly when my mother died, and it was good to see him doing so well again. I still miss her joyful greetings and her simple delight in being alive.

The days grew longer, and the air filled with singing birds; everything was fresh and clean. The trees budded with new leaves. The green velvet carpet of tender new grasses tasted delicious and the mud was warm from the brilliant sun. It felt good to see everyone. Alberta, Maggie, and Ernie ran to greet me as I lumbered toward the mighty oak near the fence, their trumpet blasts eagerly welcoming me. Hank and Edward nodded a greeting and grazed on the tender morsels of fresh bark as Yogi and BooBoo followed them everywhere. Calpurnia, Portia, Anna, and Edna stopped foraging and trumpeted their hellos, then went back to feasting on the tender new grasses. Bart trumpeted a friendly hello and disappeared into the bowels of the forest to join the boys.

I stretched my legs and fed on the fresh green leaves from an early-blooming bush. It was still too cool to swim, but the ladies rolled around in a thick warm mud-wallow. I breathed in the crisp spring air, happy again to be alive.

25

THE LAST ELEPHANT

A good friend is a connection to life—
a tie to the past, a road to the future,
the key to sanity in a totally insane world.
—LOIS WYSE

THE SUMMER DAYS were hot and heavy as we heard distant thunder, but no rain for several days. Lots of ear flapping to stay cool, and no breeze.

The moon glowed brightly in the still air one night. One of the brooks nearby trickled softly. I could see my shadow in the moonlight. Ernie snorted, trumpeted, and tore up roots. I could see the shadows of squirrels, but not the squirrels themselves. The crickets and frogs began their nightly competition. Little rabbits zigzagged across the open field and scurried into the woods. I noticed two cats in a tree, eyeing the birds, so I trumpeted loudly to scare the birds away. One of the cats glared at me, and I wondered if he was the one I kicked across the fence. I saw a family of deer grazing near the edge of the forest, four adults and three tiny fawns. A wave of sadness washed over me as I thought again that none of us will ever reproduce. Eve and Edward explained it all to me and Maggie shortly after she arrived.

Edward rumbled thoughtfully, "Mr. William, wise soul that he is, kindly provided us the opportunity to live as close to our natural habitat as possible in captivity. Those of us born in the wild can never go back to our homes far away. We have been gone too long and could not survive in the wild. And those of us who were captive born could never survive in the wild. We are not indigenous to this part of the world. The winters are much too cold. There are no heated barns in the wild or unlimited piles of bananas. We are here to live out our captive lives with as much autonomy and dignity as possible. Mr. William knows who we are and what we need. He appreciates our intelligence, wisdom, compassion, kindness, and humor. He knows how vulnerable we are and respects us as elephants. He carved out a place in the world where we can finally be ourselves."

"He is a rare human indeed,"' I rumbled.

"What is the point of breeding more elephants into captivity? We are designed to walk and eat up to eighteen hours a day. Our diet consists of bark, dirt, fruit, grass, twigs, and bamboo. We cannot forage in our barren cement prisons. There is nothing natural about cement and chains!" Eve added, snorting her disapproval.

"Cement and chains are so depressing," Maggie added sadly and flapped her oversized ears.

Edward trumpeted, "There is not a zoo in the world big enough for an elephant."

"And think of those of us who continue to live alone and isolated." Eve paused respectfully. "We are lucky to live and function as close to a family as possible, however dysfunctional. Considering none of us are related, we are fortunate to have some sort of elephant society. We live as elephants and do elephant things! We have friends and love. We are not alone, nor lonely."

"A solitary elephant without family or friends is not really an elephant!" Edward's trunk lashed like the tail of the angry cat I kicked over the fence.

"Ernie will probably outlive all of us. He will be the last elephant," I rumbled sadly, glancing at Maggie.

"Better in the forest alone than anywhere in captivity," she mused.

"Better *one day* in the forest than a lifetime in captivity," Edward and Eve said in chorus.

"Ernie's memories of all who love him will sustain him. We will teach him what he needs to know to survive happily in this place. He will never be lonely because we will always be with him in his memory," Eve rumbled consolingly.

"We must teach him everything we know!" I added enthusiastically.

Maggie burst into tears and reached for me with her trunk. Eve continued, "Let us accept what life has to offer us by living in the present and finding value in each precious moment. All we have is today."

I looked into her tired eyes and felt her wisdom.

"These are the good old days," Edward rumbled.

***

I HEARD THEM before I saw them; shrieks and squeals of laughter came from the shallow mud pond. Ernie, Yogi, BooBoo, and Hank slipped and slid in the thick mud. Ernie tried to stand up, and his legs slipped out from under him. He lay on his back, his legs waving in the air. Each time Yogi or BooBoo tried to stand, the other would knock his legs out from under him. Hank moved out of the way, basking in the sun at the side of the pond. It all seemed so natural to me I did not question Ernie being on our side of the fence until Maggie frantically trumpeted to him from her side. Naughty Ernie wiggled his little body through the bottom rung of the fence. Edna and Anna watched him from a distance, amused.

"He was so determined, we didn't have the heart to stop him," Edna confessed to Maggie later as Ernie ravenously suckled. "Besides, it is the natural order of things for him to seek out companionship other than that of his mother."

Maggie, more worried than mad, rumbled her forgiveness. The next morning after breakfast, Ernie wiggled his way through the fence and back in the mud to play with the boys.

"One of these days he's going to get stuck," Eve laughed. He never did. He wiggled through the same area most days and wore down the dirt to create an indentation that accommodated his growing body. Maggie insisted he stay near her most of the day, and they spent hours and hours in the mud together with Alberta and the other ladies. We elephants really do love our mud, and it had become close to impossible to keep Ernie out of it.

***

Maggie and I both captive born were well aware our fate depended on humans. As Eve pointed out, "It is humans who got us into this mess, and only humans can get us out."

The web of captivity is ugly. Sweet Maggie still believes humans are basically good despite everything she has been through. Without Mr. William and Ms. Hope, I shudder to think what kind of life the residents at the forest would be living today—that is, if we would even still be alive. When I look at Edward, Eve, Edna, and Bart, it is hard for me to believe that humans are basically good. I remembered what Frankie told me a long time ago, "There are many types of humans. There are good, kind, thoughtful humans like Mr. William, who genuinely care about us and our well-being, then there are also bad, cruel humans who have no business in the company of elephants—or any creature, for that matter. There are many foolish humans—careless, useless, and ignorant to the ways of elephants. They think they are helping us, but they are not."

Humans say they love us. But what do they mean by love? They do not respect us for who and what we are. How can they truly love us if they let us suffer in cages?

I remembered Rosemary, Mary, Lillian, Izzie, and Suzanna, who perished at the hands of humans. What about Jackson, Beatrice, and Little Andy? How can Maggie believe humans are basically good?

26

THESE ARE THE GOOD OLD DAYS

*A Friend may well be reckoned
the masterpiece of Nature.*
—RALPH WALDO EMERSON

EVE, MAGGIE, AND I did not talk about my mother for a very long time after her death. It was too painful. One rainy afternoon, Eve rumbled through tears, "It is an honor to have known someone who was so hard to say good-bye to. Her absence has left a big hole in all our hearts."

At forty years old, I weighed a little less than six tons. My body was muscular and physically powerful from daily exercise and proper diet. I never felt better in my life. Since I was still growing, I wondered if I would get bigger than Frankie or as big as Edward.

One night, with everyone asleep, Eve and I enjoyed the quiet under a not-quite-full moon. A solitary star twinkled brightly in the dark sky. "Listen," Eve murmured. I did not hear anything. We grazed awhile in silence. A solitary butterfly landed on the tip of my trunk. "I don't remember ever seeing a butterfly at night," she rumbled thoughtfully.

"Can you hear that?" Eve's ears were spread wide.

"Hear what? I cannot hear anything."

"Listen to the quiet, can you hear it?"

"Indeed I can!" I exclaimed.

"Stubbs is visiting. Shhhhh."

I missed my mother terribly.

"Love outlives our earthly lives and lingers inside us after everything else has faded away. It is what we leave behind that is woven into the lives of others. Your mother lives inside you and me forever, Ernest."

***

LITTLE ERNIE CONTINUED to grow. At five years old he already weighed three tons. Too big to fit under the fence anymore, he wandered away from his mother for longer periods of time. She kept her eye on his whereabouts and always knew exactly where he was. He took a shine to Alberta who returned his affection warmly. Edna insisted on her daily dose of Ernie. She shared her bananas and enjoyed his sampling whatever she was eating right out of her mouth. Anna watched, amused.

Alberta and Ernie became great friends. She lay in the middle of the shallow mud pond; he climbed and rolled all over her. When I was Ernie's age, I had never seen mud. My first experience with it was when I was almost eight and I met Maggie in paradise. I often wondered which is worse—to be captive born and never know natural elephant behaviors and what it is truly like to be an elephant, or to be taken from the wild knowing what it is like to truly be an elephant and have that taken away and not be allowed to display natural behaviors. It is hard to explain an elephant's love for mud. I suppose I could compare it to a fish's love for water. Mud is essential to our survival, without it we are incomplete as elephants. I thought of Mary and wished she were here, if only to wallow in the mud for days on end. Her elephantness would have loved it!

***

DURING ONE OF our evening visits around the fence, Eve shared her memories of the wild with Edward. Yogi and BooBoo listened, wide-eyed. Maggie, Alberta, Hank, and I always loved to hear stories about the wild. Ernie did not understand the difference, which was probably a good thing, and went to the mud with Anna and Edna. Edna never could keep her trunk off Ernie.

Eve sighed and rumbled softly, "Hundreds and hundreds of us from different families all roamed the forest far and wide along the migratory paths of our ancestors the last several thousand years. The land was plentiful, the vegetation slightly different from what is here in the forest, and there were many more sources of water. The weather changed with the seasons, but it never got as cold as here. And hot, it could get uncomfortably hot. Deep rivers always flowed that we played in, and sometimes we crossed them to the other side. I remember enjoying a mud-bath from a small puddle created after the spring rains when I was little. The adults cooled themselves with the fresh spring water as I wrestled in the mud with my sisters. We lived with wild abandon as we uprooted trunkfuls of grass with our great feet as they scraped at the earth. I will forever wonder what happened to my family and wonder if they miss me as much as I miss them."

"How could they not?" Edward affectionately insisted.

***

I HAD LIVED in the forest for almost twenty years before I knew Edward had been born in the wild and captured when he was almost four years old. He had seen the murder of his entire family. Devastated, he stood crying next to his mother's dead body for days. Weak and exhausted when the humans found him, they took him away kicking and screaming. That is all I know and it was Eve who shared his story with me one warm sleepless night.

"Poor Edward. Why did the humans kill his family?"

"The humans wanted their ivory. They hacked off their faces for their tusks," Eve snorted and her good eye flashed bitterly.

"I do not understand humans at all," I sighed, and rubbed each of my tusks with my trunk.

"Don't even try, Ernest. Don't even try."
We grazed in silence until the sun came up.

***

DEEP IN THE woods with Hank and Ernie, we recognized
the vibrations of a big truck. We made our way to the
barn to join the others, feeling apprehensive and excited about whoever might be joining us. By the time
we arrived, the rest of the group watched as Ms. Hope
and Mr. William coaxed a young mother and her small
son into the holding area. The mother was very petite,
smaller than my mother, and extremely terrified, her
eyes wide with fear. From where I stood, I guessed
the youngster to be a little younger than Ernie, who
was now a rambunctious ten-year-old. Eve, Alberta,
and Maggie reached out to the newcomer through the
fence. Her trunk wrapped tightly around her son, she
made eye contact with Eve, who held her gaze.

The mother and her young son appeared to be
in pretty good physical shape. Both slightly underweight, they devoured the hay and bananas Ms. Hope
and Mr. William left in the holding area. They remained
standoffish and kept to themselves most of the time.
For the longest time, Gracie, the mother, would only
talk to Eve and Edward upon her release from the
holding area. Bo, small for his age, turned out to actually be a couple years older than Ernie. Twelve years
old when he arrived, it did not take long for him to fill
out and catch up to Ernie in size. Handsome, though
with only one tusk, he stayed with his mother less than

a year before he came over to the male side of the forest. He immediately bonded with the boys, Owen and Oscar, and the three of them would disappear for days at a time into the bowels of the forest. Ernie took a shine to Bo but continued to tag along with Yogi and BooBoo who continued to follow Edward all over the place. When he allowed it of course.

Neither Gracie nor Bo had ever been out at night unsupervised and it took months to get them to leave the barn. Terrified of the dark, they stood overwhelmed at the barn's exit. Week after week, they remained too paralyzed to move. Under the protective and loving care of Eve, Portia, and Calpurnia, they were finally coaxed out. During the third full moon, a few hours before dawn, the ladies convinced the pair to accompany them to the fence. The moon was bright and they could see far and wide. Edward, Hank, and I stood at the fence in anticipation. Ears flapping, we all breathed a sigh of relief and listened to the earth's nightly music. The sun rose a few hours later to the morning songs of the earth. Captivity takes its toll in so many ways. Gracie and Bo had never lived on elephant time. But it only took once. They never went back to the barn again, preferring to spend every night sleeping under the stars.

I still do not know much about Gracie and Bo's lives before they arrived at the forest. I am not sure if they shared their story with Eve and Edward or not. All I know is Gracie gave birth to Bo when she was almost fifty years old and they had never been apart. It took well over a year for Gracie to reach out to any of the other elephants besides Eve and Edward. Living at the forest for a little over three years, she now spent most of her time in the company of Calpurnia and Portia. When Bo went over to the male side of the forest, she became despondent for months. Eve, Calpurnia, and Portia helped her through that difficult time, and Bo checked in with her almost every day when not exploring his new home with his new friends. Gracie smiled more these days and I noticed how beautiful she looked when her eyes sparkled. Bo was now taller than his mother. Now that my mother was gone, Gracie was the most petite of all the females and the first to arrive at the fence when Edward would show up for his weekly visit.

When she was not hungry, Gracie amused herself by throwing clumps of bananas into the air and watching them fall back to the ground. Calpurnia and Portia laughed at her and ate all the fallen bananas— that is, if Anna did not snatch them up first.

***

AFTER SPENDING ONE entire day in the woods with Hank, Ernie, Yogi, and BooBoo, I lumbered toward the fence to rest. At twenty-seven years old, the boys were boisterous, lively, and mischievous. Hank, at thirty-three was worn out, but not as much as me at forty-two years old. I lie down near the fence and saw two ducks mating near the pond. I rolled over and watched two rabbits mating under a bush. It was definitely early spring.

When Maggie plodded to the fence to check on Ernie, I asked her what ever happened to Ernie's father.

"I never met Ernie's father," she answered with the most disarmingly innocent face.

"How can that be?" I asked, confused.

"He was conceived through a tube."

"A tube?"

"Yes, a tube."

I grew impatient. "Come on Maggie, you are talking crazy."

"Ernest, the humans impregnated me with a long tube. I did not mate with an elephant!"

I glanced at Little Ernie who rolled around in the mud with Alberta. "I do not understand."

Maggie flapped her oversized ears and sighed, "It was most unpleasant."

"Oh Maggie, what happened?"

Eve, within hearing distance, lumbered closer and joined our conversation. "I heard of an elephant who had a tube stuck in her privates fourteen times. Fourteen times! She became pregnant after the ninth time and lost the baby early in her pregnancy. The twelfth time, pregnant again, she carried the baby full term, only to give birth to a dead baby boy. I heard she was devastated. The humans couldn't leave well enough alone, and performed the extremely invasive procedure two more times."

"It was humiliating, the humans stuck long tubes into my private parts!" Maggie snorted her indignation. "I couldn't get away because my legs were chained. They drew blood from my ear every day trying to determine the exact time for the procedure."

Eve flapped her ears and snorted, "In the wild we know exactly the right time and exactly what to do. Captivity throws our systems out of kilter. The humans need to leave us alone."

Maggie continued, "The procedure required me to stand very still for a long period of time."

"Sounds complicated," I grumbled. I started to ask what was in the tube and decided not to. I did not want to know. "Did it hurt?"

Maggie replied thoughtfully, "No, not exactly. It was extremely uncomfortable, though, and very embarrassing."

"The elephant I heard about did give birth to a live baby girl after her fourteenth procedure. Unfortunately the baby died after six months," Eve said softly, and shook her head sadly.

"I guess I was lucky; it only took one time for me. And Ernie appears healthy," Maggie sighed and flapped her oversized ears.

I was sorry I had asked about Ernie's father. I wondered if Edna and Anna ever gave birth, with or without a male elephant. Had Calpurnia and Portia? I wondered if Eve ever mated. I did not have the nerve to ask any of them. If they wanted me to know, they would tell me. Even today, I still try to wrap my mind around the idea that a female elephant in captivity can reproduce without a male elephant.

I remembered Eve had told me, in the wild an elephant will not reproduce during a drought or dangerous times. "An elephant knows when the time is right. Humans are unwise to go against the natural order of things," she said with an ominous rumble.

***

ONE RAINY AFTERNOON while under the oak trees, Eve explained to Ernie and me how our dung reseeds the forest to create new trees and bushes. Edward showed us how our giant feet create well-worn paths for the smaller animals to navigate through the forest. I began to understand the interconnectedness of all living things and my place in the natural order of things. From the colors of fall to the fragrance of spring, there is a cycle of nature.

The following morning the air was full of singing birds in the fresh clean brilliance of a new day. I saw Mr. William and Ms. Hope moving straw near the barn. Bachelor's Forest has given me a taste of how the world could be, though there is still a lot that needs to be done. Eve always said performing made her feel so undignified. "It was so unnatural and so unelephant!" She would trumpet loudly. "With grace and determination we will overcome our pasts," she would then snort and stomp her foot like Mary used to do. My mind wandered to the elephants still trapped in the web of captivity all alone without hope. I felt sad for them.

***

Bo JOINED HANK, Ernie, and me one particularly hot summer, and we spent our days deep in the woodlands. Another scorching summer, Edward also spent most of his days in the dense woods. As we ventured deep into the forest, we found him standing over the skeletal remains of a dead animal. He gently caressed each bone as he turned them over with his trunk. He never looked up, and when we got close he rumbled, "Robert."

"Robert?" Hank and I asked in unison.

Edward sighed, "Yes, remember Robert and Grayson?"

"My mother told me about them but that was before my time at the forest and over twenty years ago," I rumbled softly.

Hank who was very young when they died rumbled, "I remember Grayson always smiled. And he couldn't feel his feet. And how Robert frantically explored the forest as if he knew his time was limited."

Edward sighed again. "Robert had about a year of freedom. How thrilled he was just to be able to walk again! Captivity robs us of our very nature. We are designed to walk great distances on a daily basis."

"Better to live one day in the forest than forever in captivity," Hank and I chimed in together.

Bo, at fourteen, had not experienced death. He had heard our stories about those who left us too soon. Ernie remembered my mother very well. No one else had died since they arrived at the forest. Mr. William and Ms. Hope had dug a large grave and buried my mother near the fence under one of the oak trees. A horrible day for Hank and me, they were kind enough to leave us alone for a few days so we could say good-bye. Now it was hard to believe my mother had been gone for almost ten years.

I remembered Rosemary's head hanging off the back of the truck, and Jackson being thrown away in a dumpster like a piece of garbage, and Beatrice being burned near the train tracks. I wondered what had become of Mary's body. Robert, Grayson, and my mother went back to the earth. "As it should be," Eve would always say.

I wondered where Suzanna and Izzie's bodies were. Hopefully they lay together somewhere deep within the forest. At least they were home. I wondered where Frankie's body had been laid to rest.

An eerie feeling to visit the dead, in silence, I respectfully caressed Robert's bones and hoped he ran somewhere free unencumbered by humans. The only sound was the slow blowing of air from Edward's trunk as we gently touched Robert's bones with our feet. Then we politely re-covered Robert's bones with dead leaves, branches, and dirt. What a waste of a life. I felt sorry I had never met him.

***

EVE AND ERNIE visited several times a day by the fence for years. Every morning Ernie hugged Edward and stole the food out of Eve's mouth before he ran off to the mud. When he first moved over to the male side of the forest, he spent most of his time following

Yogi and BooBoo around. When he was not following them everywhere, he spent time with Hank and me. Maggie, the nervous mother, liked to know his whereabouts. Eve told her to let him go.

"Let him be the elephant he is, Maggie. He needs to be self-reliant, as he will more than likely outlive all of us."

"Maybe Bo will be the last elephant," Maggie mused.

"In the wild, the mothers insist their adolescent sons learn the ways of male society. Yet they are there to pick up the pieces when necessary. He knows you love him, Maggie. He knows you will be there for him. Let him grow up."

"I know Eve, I know. It's hard though. I am afraid for him, and I don't why."

"This is as good as it gets in captivity. Be thankful he didn't end up like Jackson!"

"Better one day in the forest than a lifetime in captivity," Maggie and I trumpeted in unison.

Eve encouraged Ernie's independence by telling him all about life in the wild. I overheard her telling him about her father late one afternoon.

"My father was known for his giant tusk. He only had one. It was over six feet long, and no other males would mess with him. He lived a solitary life most of the time, but every now and then he would come visit my mother and me. One day he stopped coming around and we never saw him again. We came upon his remains shortly before I was captured. His tusk was gone as well as his face. My mother told me he had been killed by the humans for his tusk. Soon afterward, my grandfather died from natural causes. He lived to be in his sixties and fathered many." Eve always spoke softly when she talked about her family.

Ernie listened attentively. For all he knew, we were in the wild. Ernie, who was now twelve years old, was a big boy. Not quite as stocky as Hank the Tank, yet he weighed almost four tons. He was almost as big as my mother full grown! He played and ate and napped and played and ate and napped all day every day. He grazed, dust-bathed, ate bark, tore branches off of trees, wallowed in the mud, and socialized. When he grew tired, he lay on the hillside for a nap. My mother was right. There is something to be said for the intense, quiet joy of being alive.

Ernie idolized Edward and could not wait to spend time with him. How he loved him! At forty-four years old, I had entered my prime and weighed almost seven tons. I had caught up with and surpassed Frankie but was still not as big as Edward. We weighed close to the same, but Edward was still taller.

As the years passed, Edward and Eve spent more and more time together at the top of the hill. At least once or twice a day they stood at the top and surveyed the panoramic view of their home. I believe, between the two of them, they had more wisdom than all the elephants I have ever known combined. Together, Edward and Eve commanded a stillness in the soul, an awe that cannot be put into words.

***

TO BE ABLE to tell our stories in the trusted company of each other has helped many of us heal. Having been brutalized in some way, most of us experienced some sort of powerlessness, overwhelming terror, helplessness, and cruelty, in the form of beatings, deprivation, or both. In our own time, when we feel safe and secure, there is no hurry. We are on elephant time.

We will heal. It takes a long time, but we are all healing in our own way. The younger elephants seem more resilient, having fewer traumas to recover from. The elders sometimes take longer so damaged is their ability to trust anyone or anything. We will eventually learn we are safe. Even that is a scary thought. Most of us who come to the forest do not even know what being safe means.

As Eve would always say, "We are not meant to travel the road to recovery alone. We need each other to heal."

When she first arrived, Anna Banana ate half and hid the rest of her food for later because she was so afraid of not being fed on a regular basis. You can imagine the surprise and wonder she felt at having 10,000 acres of unlimited food!

As soon as I saw Mr. William that day at the zoo, I knew my life had forever changed. I do not know why we were chosen to be the fortunate ones, but fortunate we are. I believe we got lucky because of all our friends who perished before us.

We will continue to tell their stories in order to honor our dead so they shall not have lived and died in vain. We have to tell their stories so it does not happen again. We are elephants; we are kind and gentle beings. We love, we cry, we grieve, we laugh. We are not possessions. We do not understand the ways of humans. We would not be living in the forest today if our comrades who came before had not perished at the hands of humans. I know with all my heart that the tortured souls and deaths of those who came before paid for my freedom.

We will never forget the cruelty inflicted on us over the years, and as we mourn the losses from that cruelty, we must *never* forget the casualties along the way. We will never forget those who perished at the hands of human ignorance and unfathomable cruelty. Every day as we heal and grow stronger, we will keep them alive in our memories and tell their stories to the others. We must keep the wild alive and carry on the spirit of those who are gone.

I am still angry Frankie never had the chance to live again as an elephant. He would be so at home in the forest as he thrived on elephant time. I feel sad he never again experienced his elephantness. Little Ernie would have loved him. And I know Frankie would have adored the little guy. He would have told him stories about his family and what it was like to be completely free and live in the wild, and how humans haven't a clue about elephants. Oh Frankie, I miss your handsome face, your sad eyes, and your big heart! But most of all, I miss your love. I hope there are lots of bananas wherever you are. I hope your deeply missed family is waiting by the watering hole when you become thirsty and there is more mud than you have skin. And most of all, I hope wherever you are there are no humans and you are free to be an elephant and do elephant things.

And Beatrice, your good friends kept you alive in their memories. I hope wherever you are you have a chance to meet Frankie. You would recognize him immediately, as he is the handsomest elephant who ever lived. I hope your hip is healed and you are far away from the cruel ways of humans. May there be an endless supply of watermelon and no humans to interrupt your pangs of hunger. May your reunion with your family be beyond your wildest elephant dreams.

Sweet Rosemary, I hope little Jackson is waiting for you, and when you find him he is covered from head to toe in mud with lots of friends to play with, far way from guns and the humans who use them. I hope he happily plays in the mud, pulls all the older elephants' tails, and runs around in never-ending fields of grass. May there be lots of trees to shade you from the hot sun and, when you see your family again, may they encircle you with their undying love. I hope Lilly, wherever she is, finds you well and the two of you spend forever together with trunks entwined, unafraid. No bull hooks, no boxcars, no beatings, just two old friends hanging out, finally able to be elephants.

And Mary, I hope wherever you are you find more food than you can possibly eat and you have rounded out nicely. And someday, when you and Eve reunite, you are able to feast with your families at a mutual watering hole. I hope you find Beatrice, Frankie, Lilly, Rosemary, and little Jackson far away from humans as you wallow in the mud, forage to your hearts' content, and hang out with your families every day. May the mud-baths reinvigorate your tired, dry skin and you once again become the beautiful elephant you once were. I hope you never feel pain or loneliness or sadness again. Maybe you and my mother will become friends. Please know you are greatly missed.

And Zeus, I hope you have become big and strong as you proudly roam the fields and forests and there is nothing or no one bigger or stronger than you. May you know kindness and respect as you drink to your heart's content and never feel hunger, despair, pain, or sorrow ever again. I hope you find Little Andy, make new friends at the watering hole, and never see another human again ever.

As we become able to look ahead, even to hope, we can rebuild a new life free from the grip of the dark side of humanity. We will never forget, but we can put these awful memories aside. As elephants, we live in the present. Today is a new day and we must find our strength in each other. Our purpose as elephants is to love and comfort one another while respecting all living beings. All life is sacred.

As our suffering comes to an end, and our sorrows fade away, most of our longings become satisfied, and an unspeakable joy fills our hearts and souls as we realize we finally have a place to call home.

EPILOGUE

*When you are sorrowful, look again in your heart,
and you shall see that in truth you are weeping for that which has been your delight.*
—KHALIL GIBRAN

WE LOST EVE earlier this year. Eve, our wise and trusted matriarch, friend, confidante, teacher, and protec-
tor, surrogate mother to many. She went peacefully.
Maggie sensed the end was near. Eve had slowed
down considerably and not eating as much or as often. Her last set of molars had worn down. She had
become weak and emaciated, a shrunken version of
her former self. She lay down under the giant oak tree
near the fence where my mother died. Maggie, Hank,
Ernie, and I were by her side. Edward paced back
and forth nearby, while Yogi and BooBoo looked on in
distress. Edna and Anna consoled Bart by the fence
while Calpurnia, Portia, Gracie, Alberta, and the boys
kept a respectful distance. Surrounded by all who
loved her, Eve took her last breath, and her grand
heart beat no more.

And how grand she was. So majestic, so kind, so calm, so wise. There will never be another Eve. The earth and the sky were sad to have lost her. It rained nonstop for over a week after she died. Even the birds did not sing for weeks after she left us.

Seventy-four years old and actually relieved to die from natural causes, which was pretty amazing after all she had been through. Eve was "proud to leave this earth as an elephant should, for even the grass wilts and the flowers fade!"

It was still hard to let her go. Little Ernie has taken her death the hardest and suffers still from the loss of his *self-appointed* godmother. He stands over her grave every day, head hung low, kicking the dirt. His loud anguished trumpets break our hearts. Maggie keeps a respectful distance and lets him grieve. Coming to terms with her absence, we all grieve in our own ways. Edward has started to reach out to the rest of us more than usual. He has become a little more social—so great is his pain. He did not stop pacing for months after he lost his good friend Eve.

Eve was a great teacher, and her lessons will live on in all of us. I can hear her say, "We must accept what life has to offer by living in the present, finding value in each precious moment."

I do not know where we go when we die. I can only hope Eve reunites with her deeply loved family. Hopefully she and Frankie will become friends. He would be seventy-two if he were still alive. Maybe Eve, Mary, Beatrice, and my mother will all come together to drink at a mutual watering hole. I do not know.

Every morning I visit Eve's grave and listen to the gentle breeze that tenderly bends the soft green grass. I hear the sound of my heart beating as the sun warms my back. A small brook trickles calmly nearby. I listen to the quiet that once was Eve.

***

I FOUND MYSELF wanting to spend more and more time alone. As the ladies socialized by the fence, I wander deep into the woods. The crisp, dry winter air pierces my lungs as I inhale. Awed by the cold moonlit beauty, I suddenly feel vulnerable. A warm mist envelopes me and I feel safe again. Out of nowhere a lone butterfly flits about and lands on the tip of my trunk. I cannot help but smile.

It is late winter, but the noonday sun is warm enough for sunbathing. The brilliant sunlight reflecting from one of the semi-frozen ponds cleanses my mind of the darkness taking hold since Eve left us. I find myself angry she is gone. I miss her. I yearn for her majestic and calming presence. I hope she finds my mother and Frankie. Somewhere deep in the recesses of my memory in a far-away place, I hear a lonely trumpet echo through the treetops like Frankie's disappearing dreams of yesterday. I kick the dirt. A small gust of warm air caresses my face. At that moment, I know with certainty I am not alone.

Later that night I look up at the dark sky and next to the moon I see a solitary star twinkling down at me. Eve lives forever inside me. I will never be alone.

***

EVERY DAY I climb up the steep hill to take in the view that delights my soul. I stand at the top and lose myself in the beauty of the forest that has become my home. From this height, I see the ladies enjoying the warm sun, ears flapping as they quietly graze. Turning to the left, I see the boys mock fighting on the other side of the fence while Bart and Hank bask in the warm sun on the side of their favorite hill. Maggie is the new matriarch. None of the older ladies were willing to step up. Maggie and Alberta lie in a warm mud-wallow not at all concerned about the cold air such is their love for mud on their skin. I see Yogi and BooBoo, now in their early thirties, dust-bathing and playing with little Ernie. He follows them almost everywhere. Kindhearted souls, they let him tag along as they continue to explore every nook and cranny of their habitat.

Aware of a presence, I realize I am not alone. Edward, now in his seventies, still looms tall over all of us. As the second largest bull, I am still no match for him. He too is taking in the sights below as we stand side by side. I enjoy his company and feel relieved to experience his newfound peace. He slept fitfully, or not at all, for months after Eve left us. He finally stopped pacing. I know he misses her as much as I do. As my mother would say, "Grief is the price we pay for love." We enjoy our quiet moments together, Edward and I; our huge hearts beat in sympathetic unison. I feel blessed to be in his gentle company.

***

I FEEL THE vibration of the big truck before I actually hear it. As is customary, we will all be there to welcome the new arrival. I start my descent down the hill. Edward falls in step and side by side we journey forward. Bart, Hank, and Ernie follow. The boys, Bo, Owen, and Oscar appear from deep within the forest, followed by Yogi and BooBoo. Maggie, Alberta, Portia, Calpurnia, and Gracie walk together along the fence toward the barn. Edna and Anna, side by side, follow not too far behind. We are all excited yet apprehensive about meeting our new comrade.

My name is Ernest, and I am a seven-ton, forty-five-year-old bull elephant. This is my story.

What though the radiance which was once so bright
Be now forever taken from my sight,
Though nothing can bring back the hour
Of splendour in the grass,
Of glory in the flower,
We will grieve not, rather find
Strength in what remains behind.
—WILLIAM WORDSWORTH

FURTHER READING AND INFORMATION

Amory, Cleveland. 1997. *Ranch of Dreams*. New York: Penguin Putnam.

Bradshaw, G. A. 2009. *Elephants on the Edge: What Animals Teach Us about Humanity.* New Haven, CT: Yale University Press.

Moss, Cynthia J., Harvey Croze, and Phyllis C. Lee. 2011. *The Amboseli Elephants: A Long-Term Perspective on a Long-Lived Mammal.* Chicago: University of Chicago Press.

Nicholson, Christopher. 2009. *The Elephant Keeper*. New York: HarperCollins.

Payne, Katy. 1998. *Silent Thunder: In the Presence of Elephants*. New York, NY: Simon & Schuster.

Ryan, R. J. 1999. *Keepers of the Ark.* USA: Xliris.

Sewell, Anna. 1877. *Black Beauty*. Great Britain: Jarrold & Sons.

Sheldrick, Daphne. 2012. *Love, Life, and Elephants: An African Love Story*. New York: Farrar, Straus and Giroux.

Watson, Lyall. 2002. *Elepantoms: Tracking the Elephant*. New York: W. W. Norton & Company.

Due Date Receipt

Sarasota County
Library System

7/16/2016

www.scgov.net/library
941-861-1110

Items checked out to

Guerrero, Jahelda

Number of item(s)   1

BARCODE 31969024425638
TITLE Through the eyes of Ernest : a memoir
  honor elephants / Debbie McFee.
DUE DATE 8/8/2016

IF YOU WANT TO HELP ELEPHANTS

www.4theelephants.com/Organizations